THE  TIMES
HOW TO DO
THE TIMES
CROSSWORD

THE TIMES

HOW TO DO THE TIMES CROSSWORD

Brian Greer

TIMES
BOOKS

Published in 2001 by Times Books
HarperCollins*Publishers*
77-85 Fulham Palace Road
Hammersmith
London W6 8JB

The HarperCollins website address is www.**fire**and**water**.com
Copies of this book can be ordered through this website.

First published in 2001 by Times Books

Reprint 10 9 8 7 6 5 4 3 2

Copyright © Brian Greer 2001

The Times is a registered trademark of Times Newspapers Ltd

ISBN 0-00-710840-0

British Library Cataloguing in Publication Data
A catalogue record for this book is available from the British Library.

Printed and bound in Great Britain by
Omnia Books Limited, Glasgow

CONTENTS

PREFACE

For five years I enjoyed the privilege of editing *The Times* Crossword. Then, in 2000, I decided to return to full-time academic life, having secured a position at San Diego State University. I work on mathematics education here, as does my wife, Swapna, to whom this book is dedicated.

On becoming crossword editor, I discovered a latent trait of authoritarianism and the truth of the saying that "All power tends to corrupt, and absolute power … is even nicer." Having been a contributor of puzzles for more than twenty years, under the mentorship of Edmund Akenhead and then John Grant, I had developed very definite ideas about an appropriate style, with which the team of contributors learned to put up with (mostly) good-humoured forbearance. Now I have happily handed over to Mike Laws, whose knowledge and love of crosswords are second to none, and who is much better equipped than I to deal with the multiple demands of the job.

Since the early 1970s, I had the pleasure of competing in, then helping to run, the annual Times Crossword Championship, superbly organised by Harold Franklin, Mike Rich and John Grimshaw. I had the chance to marvel at the prowess of John Sykes, Roy Dean and many other great solvers, and the honour, on occasions, of seeing them dispose of my carefully constructed puzzles in minutes.

In this book I have tried to systematise the principles that guided my editing in a way that will help solvers. With my strong predilection for examples, I have included a large number of clues for the reader to tackle. Most of these have been taken from a haphazard collection of my own *Times* puzzles. Some are great clues from other

Times setters, mostly extracted from my imperfect memory, and I hope that their creators will forgive me for not crediting them. Since, when solving clues under normal conditions, one expects to have letters available from intersecting answers, I have included a "First Aid Section" (p. 111) wherein, if you cannot solve a clue, you can find some of the letters and try again with that help before resorting to the Solutions and Notes (p. 117)

There are also five complete crosswords in Chapter 3 that illustrate the evolution of *Times* style since the first crossword in 1930. At the ends of Chapters 5, 8 and 10 are three more for revision purposes. Their solutions will also be found at the end of the book.

I will continue to enjoy the intellectual challenge of setting and solving crosswords, encouraged by the evidence that it helps to maintain active mental life, but now I am struggling with puzzles of a different sort, namely what prevents children from understanding mathematics, and why do so many people fear and hate it.

BRIAN GREER
SAN DIEGO, FEBRUARY 2001

Chapter 1
IN THE BEGINNING

BIRTH OF THE CROSSWORD

December 21, 1913 is generally accepted as the date of the first crossword, and Arthur Wynne is credited as its creator. Wynne was an emigrant from England to the United States who was working as editor of the "Fun" supplement of the *New York Sunday World*. For the Christmas issue of that year, he was looking for an innovation for a section that presented readers with traditional puzzles such as rebuses, riddles, and anagrams.

The puzzle he devised was diamond-shaped (with a diamond-shaped hole in the middle) and was called "Word-Cross". Each clue was referenced by two numbers in the first and last squares of the answer's location in the grid. Notwithstanding these differences in appearance from what we are familiar with today, it had the essential features of a crossword, namely different sets of intersecting words reading horizontally and vertically to be worked out from clues.

As a puzzle form, the crossword had many antecedents with long histories, particularly acrostics, word-squares and word diamonds (for more details, refer to the books by Michelle Arnot, Roger Millington, and Tony Augarde cited in this chapter). Wynne himself acknowledged the influence of puzzles in children's magazines that he read as a child in Liverpool. Indeed, Roger Millington, in his book *The Strange World of the Crossword* (M. & J. Hobbs, 1974), reproduced such a puzzle from 1880 in the shape of a diamond, with clues divided into "Across" and "Downward", that seems to have as much claim to being a crossword as Wynne's "Word-Cross". According to older editions of *The Guinness Book of Records*, the first crossword – also diamond-shaped – appeared in *St Nicholas* children's magazine in New York City in September 1875.

Despite the negative reaction of his colleagues, and unanticipated by Wynne himself, Word-Cross evoked enough interest among readers to be repeated and become a regular feature. By the middle of January, 1914, the name had been transposed to "Cross-Word", with subtitle "Find the missing cross words".

The next ten years saw steady if unspectacular progress, and improvements in format. The hyphen was dropped from the name. From July 22, 1923, clues were referenced more simply by a single number in the first square of the answer (a simplification suggested by a crossword enthusiast who called himself "Radical"). Symmetry in the grid was accepted as standard. It became the norm to have a grid in which every letter is checked, ie, belongs to both an across word and a down word – a criterion that is followed by American crosswords to this day.

The transformation of a popular American pastime into a national craze was significantly accelerated by the appearance in 1924 of the first crossword puzzle book from a new publishing house launched by a pair of recent graduates called Simon and Schuster. The first printing sold out within twenty-four hours, and almost half a million of the first three puzzle volumes were sold within a year. In a foreword, F. Gregory Hartswick wrote that "The cross word [sic] solver becomes a collector, a connoisseur of words. They lose, to him, their mundane purpose of a suitable medium for the exchange of thoughts, and take on an esoteric significance, akin to the appeal of slip-ware to the collector of pottery or the three-cornered Mauritius to the philatelist". The clues, by the way, were still labelled, following Wynne's terminology, as "horizontal" and "vertical".

The extent to which the crossword captured public consciousness and affected every aspect of life during the succeeding years is thoroughly documented in Michelle Arnot's *A History of the*

Crossword Puzzle (Macmillan, 1982), Millington's book already cited, and *The Oxford Guide to Word Games* by Tony Augarde (Oxford University Press, 1986). Arnot reports, for example, a case in Chicago in which a "crossword widow" sued for severance on the grounds that her husband was spending too much time solving crosswords and neglecting his financial duties; the judge ruled that he limit himself to three puzzles a day. To Augarde's book I am indebted for the information that a revue on Broadway in 1925 called *Puzzles* included a scene in a "Crossword Puzzle Sanatorium" for people who had been driven insane by the craze. On January 1, 1925 the cover of the *Saturday Evening Post* by Norman Rockwell, whose illustrations for that magazine chronicled American life for nearly fifty years, showed two men working on a crossword. (A more recent work on the same topic is David Hockney's composite photograph *The Crossword Puzzle Minneapolis Jan. 1983*, showing Martin and Mildred Friedman working together on an American crossword.)

The enduring prominence of the crossword in American culture is illustrated by its recent philatelic appearance. When the US Post Office issued sets of stamps to commemorate each decade of the 20th century, Arthur Wynne's pioneering effort was featured for the 1910s, alongside such other notable events as the First World War, the Panama Canal, and Charlie Chaplin.

CROSSING THE POND

From the other side of the Atlantic, the "Thunderer" regarded the phenomenon with Olympian disdain. In December, 1924, under the headline "An Enslaved America" it reported that "All America has succumbed to the crossword puzzle" and characterized the crossword as "a menace because it is making devastating inroads on the working hours of every rank of society". The New York correspondent estimated that Americans spent five million hours daily on crosswords, many of them during "working" hours. The deadly virus had already been transmitted, however, in the form of puzzles from

Arthur Wynne that appeared, slightly adapted, in the *Sunday Express* (indeed, a crossword was published in *Pearson's Magazine* in 1922). Two months after its original pronouncement, *The Times* ruefully admitted that its comments were "hardly printed before the craze had crossed the Atlantic with the speed of a meteorological depression".

By this time, the fad had already gained the approval of some very top people. *The New York Times* was delighted to report Queen Mary's enjoyment of crosswords and Stanley Baldwin told the audience at a Press Club luncheon:

> I as Prime Minister and you as journalists are engaged in the common work of trying to elevate the people of this country, and you are doing it today through that marvellous medium, the crossword puzzle. There is now hardly a man, woman or child in this country who is not familiar with the name of Eli. The fact that Asa was King of Judah can be concealed now from none. I should think that ninety per cent of the people believe that there was but one Roman Emperor and that his name was Nero. They have learned that there is a mysterious bird in a far country of three letters and one snake of three letters.

By 1927, as Tony Augarde in *The Oxford Guide to Word Games* puts it, only a learned judge could be unaware of the crossword, as reflected in the following interchange from A. P. Herbert's *Misleading Cases in the Common Law* (in passing, the extent to which crosswords have interacted with the law is worthy of note):

> *Sir Antony Dewlap*: The action is unusual … by reason of the channel which the defendant has selected for his abuse. Melud, that channel is no other than the innocent and familiar 'Cross-word' …
> *Mr Justice Snubb*: What is that?
> *Sir Antony Dewlap*: Forgive me, melud. Melud, with great respect, melud, a cross-word puzzle is a form of puzzle,

melud, in which a number of numbered squares in a
chequered arrangement of – er – squares, melud, have to be
filled in with letters, melud, these letters forming words,
melud, which words are read both horizontally and vertically,
melud – that is, both across and down, if your lordship
follows me – and which words may be deduced from certain
descriptions or clues, which are provided with the puzzle,
melud, these descriptions having numbers, melud, which are
to be. filled in with the correct letters and words according to
the descriptions which have the corresponding numbers,
melud, whether horizontally or vertically, as the case may be.
Does you lordship follow me?
Mr Justice Snubb: No.

Adrian Bell, in his foreword to *The Penguin Book of The Times
50th Anniversary Crosswords* (1980) described the circumstances
which led *The Times* to conclude that what could not be beaten must
perforce be joined. Although most crosswords available to the British
public were of the straightforward definitional type – "still a toy for
vacant minds" in Bell's terms – a rival at the same price of two pence
was publishing something more substantial and thereby gaining in the
circulation battle with *The Times*. Towards the end of 1929, the assistant
editor of *The Times* told Adrian Bell's father, Robert, who was News
Editor and also crossword setter for *The Observer*, that *The Times*
would have to start a crossword puzzle and asked if he knew of
anyone who could do the job. Robert Bell volunteered his son.

In order to gauge reaction, the first crosswords Adrian Bell
created appeared in *The Times Weekly Edition*, beginning on January 2,
and two of them were reprinted in The Times on January 23 and 30.
The response was sufficiently encouraging that the official
"Crossword Puzzle No 1" was launched in *The Times* on February 1,
1930. Fifty years later to the day, the crossword to celebrate the
Golden Jubilee was the work of the same remarkable author.
Both puzzles are reproduced in Chapter 3, where I survey the stylistic
development of *The Times* crossword over that period.

EMERGENCE AND DEVELOPMENT OF THE BRITISH CRYPTIC

Following the popularisation of the crossword in the United States and its importation to Britain, it spread so widely across cultures that today crossword puzzles, of varying forms and styles, can be found in virtually every language in the world that has a written form. Almost immediately, contrasting subspecies began to evolve on either side of the Atlantic. While, to this day, the standard American puzzle relies mainly on definitional clues (albeit often very amusingly misleading), the British crossword developed into the familiar cryptic puzzle of today, adapting many features of earlier types of puzzles and long-established forms of wordplay and linguistic humour.

Within the British environment, a further broad subdivision may be noted between the standard daily cryptics best exemplified in the daily puzzles of *The Times* and its competitors, and a divergent tradition of erudite and extremely difficult puzzles. The latter tradition began with such revered pioneers as A. F. Ritchie and Edward Powys Mathers. Ritchie took as his pseudonym "Afrit", which apart from being part of his name, means a sort of demon. Calling himself "Torquemada", Mathers initiated the *Observer* tradition of pseudonyms from the Spanish Inquisition, carried on by Derrick Somerset Macnutt ("Ximenes") and into the present by Jonathan Crowther ("Azed", derived from Don Diego de Deza). Their puzzles are characterised by arcane vocabulary (*Chambers Dictionary* being the Authorised Version), reliance on extremely wide knowledge, particularly of literature, and the use of diagrams in which words are separated by bars rather than black squares. I vividly remember my first encounter with a Ximenes puzzle, arduously constructing the answer ELEEMOSYNARY, and then verifying that this unlikely combination of letters is, indeed, a word of the English language.

The *Listener* series, which has multiple contributors, began in 1930 and survived when the BBC discontinued its parent publication in 1991, being taken over by *The Times*. It is remarkable for the variety and difficulty of its puzzles, which take many geometrical forms, including three-dimensional, present diverse forms of clue, and require answers in many forms. In the past, for example, some puzzles were in Greek, and mathematical puzzles remain an occasional feature. Among those considering the *Listener* crossword the greatest (with *The Times* daily cryptic second) was Leonard Bernstein.

Afrit established what is generally regarded as the most fundamental principle of fair play, which has come to be known as "Afrit's Injunction". In his book *Armchair Crosswords* (Warne, 1949), he wrote as follows (note that *The Book of the Crossword* was not an actual work, but rather a virtual "exhaustive treatise"):

> We must expect the composer to play tricks, but we shall insist that he play fair. *The Book of the Crossword* lays this injunction upon him: "You need not mean what you say, but you must say what you mean." This is a superior way of saying that he can't have it both ways. He may attempt to mislead by employing a form of words which can be taken in more than one way, and it is your fault if you take it the wrong way, *but it is his fault if you can't logically take it the right way.*

Afrit was echoing the Mad Hatter, who pointed out to Alice that to say that "I mean what I say" means the same as "I say what I mean" is as illogical as to say that "I see what I eat" means the same as "I eat what I see".

In *Ximenes on the Art of the Crossword* (Methuen, 1966), Macnutt established principles of clue construction that have come to be known as "Ximenean", and constitute an orthodoxy among the setters and solvers of *Listener* and Azed puzzles. Many, but by no means all, of the Ximenean rules, are accepted among those whose preference is the standard daily cryptic. One major area of disagreement is that Ximeneans are extremely permissive in what they accept as an anagram indicator, provided it is a verb or an adjective. On the other hand, they consider that nouns should not be used as anagram indicators, for example they would not allow "confusion" to take this role in the following clue (which I regard as acceptable):

Friend found in much confusion (4)

Returning to the realm of standard daily cryptics, there are three excellent precursors to the present book that lay out the general principles of clue construction. The earliest is *Anatomy of the Crossword* by Douglas St. P. Barnard (Bell, 1963). His analysis of clue types is presented with elaborate terminology, of which an extreme example is the description of:

Presumably it would house a lady as well as a lord (5)

as "an Allusive Dilemmatic Amphibological Concomitant Parabole", which he justifies as a concise (!) way of referring to "A clue which does not define but which alludes to the purpose of the light provided it be read in a certain way, and which, if read in a different way describes a logical extension of the idea which could be expressed by the light if, instead of being regarded as a whole word, the light were to be considered as two words and a rational meaning were to be ascribed to the phrase so formed" ("light" means the answer to the clue). Fortunately, as he acknowledges, it is not necessary for a solver to become familiar with such technical terminology and those who find such sesquipedalian coinages forbidding rather than intriguing can easily ignore them and enjoy his analysis of a wide range of ingenious clues.

Barnard's book offers also many reflections on the nature of the strange game between setter and solver in which the former, having made the first move, subsequently makes no interventions. He also offers a psychological explanation for the popularity of crosswords:

It is strange that in a world beset by real problems of inescapable clamancy, man should choose to set himself still more problems in the form of patterns and clues. Perhaps it is a sign of human perversity. On the other hand, it may be that he finds it a welcome challenge to grapple occasionally with some challenge which, unlike so many of the world's problems, really can be met – something which really has got an answer, and can be solved …

Barnard also argues that cryptic crosswords are beneficial in encouraging independent thinking: "If the cryptic solver is to achieve any reasonable success, he must train himself to distrust the obvious, to free his mind from misconceptions, to reject face-values, and to be dissatisfied with conventional responses".

A less flamboyant, but in many ways technically sounder, guide is *Crosswords* by Alec Robins (Teach Yourself Books, Hodder & Stoughton, 1975), revised as *The ABC of Crosswords* (Corgi, 1981). Like many other setters, I ingested many of the principles of clue construction from this book, and benefited greatly from its precision. As a good example of the attention to detail, consider this attempt:

I am included in the plan, it's obvious (5)

Many a beginner would consider this an acceptable clue. As Robins pointed out, however, what you are saying is that the letter "I" *is* included in the word "plan", so "I am" does not work. It is a flaw easy enough to remedy, for example by changing the clue to:

I must be included in the plan, it's obvious (5)

Another telling example is the following:

A limb and an associate, in a lawful manner (7)

It has the structure of a sound clue, and all the components are there (LEG + ALLY = LEGALLY). However, like the grammatically correct sentence used as an example by the linguist Noam Chomsky "Green ideas sleep furiously", it doesn't make much sense.

Like Robins, I consider it obligatory on the setter to provide a clue that is not only technically sound, but also makes coherent sense.

Robins summed up the clue-writer's duty thus:

Firstly, he must be prepared to take infinite pains in revising his work so that careless slips and slovenly constructions are eliminated ... Secondly, he must constantly remind himself that he is taking part in a game for entertainment only, and that his aim is not to concoct clues which will defy solution but those which will stimulate thought, challenge ingenuity and finally yield, if possible to the accompaniment of an appreciative chuckle by the solver... Lastly, and perhaps of greatest importance, he must ensure that the information he does give, however cleverly camouflaged for the purpose of misleading, is absolutely accurate and that he really does say with complete clarity what the answer means, so that the solver, once he has worked out the clue, can be certain that his answer is the unique one which satisfies all the conditions. To sum up, he must give his solvers faith, help and clarity, and perhaps the greatest of these is clarity.

The third major work in the genre is *Chambers Crossword Manual* (Chambers, 1986, and reprinted since, including in paperback) by Don Manley, a prolific setter, editor, and analyst of crosswords over many years, whose work continues to appear in many publications, including *The Times*. His systematic guide shows, with exemplary clarity, how the various clue types have as precise a structure as an algebraic equation or a Latin sentence.

Manley follows Afrit's injunction, mentioned above, that "You need not mean what you say, but you must say what you mean" and is an avowed "Ximenean" in the sense defined above. As an example of an unfair clue, he cites:

An accomplishment indeed to be beaten (8)

The supposed build-up is FEAT within DEED, but there is a difference between "indeed" and "in deed". I agree, and as *Times* Crossword Editor, I did not allow the use of such devices. In general, I take the view that whether such licence is permitted or not is, like bidding in bridge, to a considerable extent a matter of convention. What is essential is that the editor of a particular crossword adheres to consistent conventions on which a regular solver can rely.

Chambers Crossword Manual covers the range from standard cryptics to the "hard stuff" of Afrit, Torquemada, Ximenes, Azed, and *The Listener*, and likewise from standard clue types to more advanced and unorthodox devices. It also includes an excellent sample of 80 crosswords from all parts of the spectrum.

All three books provide extensive guidance on how to solve crosswords, to which, in the next chapter, I begin to add mine.

Chapter 2
LEARNING HOW TO
SOLVE CROSSWORDS

THE SETTER AND THE SOLVER

In *The Torquemada Puzzle Book* (Victor Gollancz, 1934), Torquemada
(E. Powys Mathers) wrote an introductory section on "How to Solve
Crosswords" that begins thus:

> If Verity, say, were to contribute an article to a Manual for
> Batsmen on How to Bowl, he would probably remain
> comparatively unread; if he wrote an article on How to Take
> My Bowling, the batsmen would read and profit. But the two
> articles, if Verity were really trying to be helpful, would be
> much the same. Assuring you at once that the analogy goes
> no further than that my wish is to help my opponent,
> I contend that the solver is more likely to read How to Solve
> Crosswords than How I Set Crosswords, though the latter title
> covers all I have to say.

> (Hedley Verity was a pre-war Yorkshire and England slow bowler.)

In undertaking to write this book of guidance for present and
future *Times* Crossword solvers, I can draw on several decades of
experience as a solver. Important though that is, I would suggest that
it is my insider experience as a setter that is more important in
sharing with you many tricks of the trade.

Another view of the symbiosis between setter and solver was
suggested by Edmund Akenhead, the Crossword Editor who guided

me through my probationary period into tenure as a setter. Setters are, he commented "of course sadists (although in the nicest possible way) and since all solvers appear to be masochists this leads to a rather beautiful relationship".

How does someone become an expert solver? In his classic *How to Solve It* (Princeton University Press, 1945) George Polya suggested that the two key ways to learn are imitation and practice. He was talking about problem-solving in mathematics, but there are interesting parallels. Polya was a crossword fan himself and makes many references to crosswords, for example that "a mathematics problem may be as much fun as a crossword puzzle" (with which I agree). He also declared that "Some time (but not too much time) spent on crossword puzzles may be quite rewarding; we can learn something about problem solving, how we think, and how we ought to think" (1965, vol. 2, p. 61), with which I also agree.

Here's an example of Polya interpreting a crossword clue mathematically:

In a crossword puzzle … we find the following clue:

This form of rash aye is no proof (7)

This is a vicious little sentence; it almost makes sense … Yet we suspect that some vague echo of a sense was put into the clue just to lead us astray. There may be a better lead: the phrase "form of" may mean "anagram of". And so we may try to interpret the clue as follows:

The unknown x is a word. The condition consists of two parts: (r1), x is an anagram of (has the same seven letters as) RASH AYE;
(r2), "x is no proof" is a meaningful (probably usual) phrase…

… and so on.

Polya suggests (vol. 1, p. 118) that a student sitting an examination can profitably ask of a question "What kind of problem is this?" If (s)he can answer that question, (s)he can apply the appropriate method for problems of that type (assuming it is known). Moreover, "the type of problem may suggest the type of solution" (p. 118). In an extreme case, there may be "key words" in the problem that act as cues telling the solver what method to apply.

Much the same applies to crossword clues. If the solver can correctly answer "What kind of clue is this?" (s)he is well on the way to finding the solution. For many standard types of clue, there are key words or other telltale indications as to which type it is. In Polya's example above, the phrase "form of" (in juxtaposition with two words with a total of seven letters) suggested an anagram. Of course, the skilful setter will slip in occasional clues with misleading cues of this sort, just as a skilful examiner can set mathematical problems in which the surface features are misleading.

Up to a point, then, you can learn how to spot an anagram, a hidden clue, and so on. In the following chapters I will instruct you, as capably as I can, about the nature of standard clues, variations upon them, and some more unusual types. Barnard, in his *Anatomy of the Crossword*, debated whether by laying bare the bones of the crossword, he might remove the mystery. He concluded, as do I, that there is no such danger. The enjoyment of bridge and chess, he pointed out, have not been diminished, but rather enhanced, by extensive analysis, and there is no reason why the same should not apply to crosswords. The resourceful setter can always keep one step ahead, just as, in mathematics, there are problems that yield to routine procedures and those that do not, many remaining unsolved after centuries.

In short, solving crosswords is partly a science and partly an art (the same applies, of course, to setting). Insofar as solving is scientific, the solver can learn and practice a repertoire of techniques that, applied to certain clues, will readily yield the answers. Insofar as it is an art, I would suggest that there are two fundamental ways of becoming an expert – the same that Polya identified as important for learning the art of mathematical problem solving, namely imitation and practice.

An excellent way to become an expert, in crosswords as in any other art, is to find a mentor, following what in current educational terminology is termed the apprenticeship model of learning.

In the absence of such a person, the study of books such as this one should, I hope, prove of considerable help, especially when starting, but the most effective method is practice, preferably daily. It is a good idea to specialise on a particular publication's crossword, since in that way you will learn a particular style. If, as I hope, your choice is *The Times* puzzle, then you will find a reasonable stylistic homogeneity imposed by the editor, notwithstanding the range of contributing setters.

As Polya wrote about solving mathematical problems, an essential step is looking back on the problem. Attempts to solve each day's puzzle must be followed by checking the answers and working out how they are derived from the clues – in a fair crossword, only the clues should puzzle you, the answers rarely. If you find that you cannot work out the explanation for an answer, try to find someone who can explain it to you – or write to the crossword editor.

EVOLUTION OF THE CRYPTIC CLUE

Crosswords exist in virtually every country of the world, with fascinating variations in structure and style. While, in the majority of cases, the clues are definitional, there are cryptic crosswords in many languages other than English, including for example, Bengali, Hebrew, and Welsh. Nevertheless, it is clear that the nature of English, especially because of its multifarious forms of ambiguity, makes it a particularly good medium for the kinds of wordplay that cryptic clues exploit.

While stylistic variations and differences in conventions are obvious to those who regularly solve crosswords in different publications, a set of largely consensual principles has developed that governs the construction of clues in the standard daily British cryptic. In particular, it is now considered essential for a clue to include a definition of the answer and a cryptic indication of that answer. With some exceptions that will be clarified later, this means that the typical clue has a two-part structure, one part being the definition and the other an alternative way of deriving the answer, the parts being juxtaposed in either order. In the rest of this chapter, I identify the historical roots of the mainstream clue types that are analysed in full in subsequent chapters, and discuss some of the "fair play" principles and conventions that govern clues in *The Times* Crossword.

While the ancestors of the form of the crossword are the word-square and the acrostic, the antecedents of cryptic clues are numerous forms of wordplay and puzzles based on words and letters. Cryptic clues may be divided into those that play with sentence meaning, those that play with word meaning, those that play with word fragments, those that play with letters, and those that play with sound.

PLAYING WITH SENTENCE MEANING

In ancient times, a notorious source of ambiguity was the oracle at Delphi. A general who wished to know whether he should go on a journey was told "Domine, stes" (Master, stay) – or was that "Domi ne stes" (at home do not stay)?

Puns take three forms, namely those based on polysemy (words that are spelled identically but have different meanings), those based on homophony (words that are pronounced identically but have different spellings) and those based on similarity of sound. Puns of the last type are literally as old as Adam, since the Hebrew words for "man" and "earth" are similar (and man was made from earth, according to Genesis). At this point, it is the first type that is relevant, while the second type will be discussed later in relation to clues that play with sound.

When Dr Johnson observed an altercation between two women leaning out of windows on opposite sides of a narrow street, he observed, "Those two will never agree, because they are arguing from different premises." Witticisms of this kind offer a source to be mined for cryptic cluing, as in the following (down) clue:

Girl's upset about serving Americans arguing on premises (9)

The ambiguity of English words and sentences has often been exploited to dramatic and poetic effect. Shakespeare, in particular, used puns extensively, as in the interchange between Hamlet and a grave-digger:

Hamlet: Whose grave's this, sirrah?
Clown: Mine, sir…
Hamlet: I think it be thine, indeed, for thou liest in't.
Clown: You lie out on't, sir, and therefore 'tis not yours. For my part, I do not lie in't, yet it is mine.
Hamlet: Thou dost lie in't, to be in't and say it is thine; 'tis for the dead, not for the quick; therefore thou liest.
Clown: 'Tis a quick lie, sir, 'twill away again from me to you.
Hamlet: What man dost thou dig it for?
Clown: For no man, sir.
Hamlet: What woman, then?
Clown: One that was a woman, sir; but rest her soul, she's dead.

Recall also the oracular utterances of the witches in *Macbeth* that misleadingly suggested him to be invulnerable.

From more recent times, Tom Stoppard's play *Professional Foul* is packed with examples showing the ambiguity and apparent illogicality of language. Here is an interchange between two philosophers flying to a conference in Prague – McKendrick is introducing himself to Professor Anderson:

> *McKendrick*: I wasn't sure it was you. Not a very good likeness.
> *Anderson*: I can assure you this is how I look.
> *McKendrick*: I mean your photograph. (*He flips his brochure open. It contains small photographs and pen portraits of various men and women who are in fact to be speakers at the colloquium.*) The photograph is younger.
> *Anderson*: It must be an old photograph.
> *McKendrick (Changing seats)*: Bill McKendrick.
> *Anderson*: How odd.
> *McKendrick*: Is it?
> *Anderson*: Young therefore old. Old therefore young. Only odd at first glance.
> *McKendrick*: Oh yes.
> *Anderson*: The second glance is known as linguistic analysis. A lot of chaps pointing out that we don't always mean what we say, even when we manage to say what we mean.

Remembering Afrit's Injunction "You need not mean what you say, but you must say what you mean", the implication is that the crossword solver must analyse the linguistic structure of clues to determine what in the clue corresponds to what the setter meant, regardless of whatever that which has been said might appear to mean.

There are many sources of ambiguous sentences, such as the supposed endorsement "I used your soap ten years ago since when I have used no other" or the possibly useful line for a reference "You will be extremely lucky if you can get this man to work for you". Nixon is supposed to have been encouraged by his mother telling him "Richard, don't you ever give up!" when, in fact, what she said was "Richard, don't you ever give up?"

From modern linguistics comes an example used by Noam Chomsky to illustrate, through ambiguity, the difference between surface structure and deep structure of language. His example:

Flying planes can be dangerous

could either mean that the flying of planes is a dangerous activity or that planes that are flying can be dangerous. A crossword clue with precisely parallel ambiguity is the following:

Hunting animals can be dear sport (9)

Another example exploiting the same type of ambiguity is:

Lock soldier up inside for hunting female (7) [D]

("[D]" after this clue indicates that it is specifically a down clue – necessary to specify in this case because of the use of "up" to indicate a reversal. Likewise "[A]" throughout will indicate an across clue).

The most usual form in which ambiguity at the sentence level is exploited by the cryptic setter is analogous to one form of riddle, defined by David Crystal in *The Cambridge Dictionary of Language* as when "objects, animals, people, and events are deliberately described in such a way that their description suggests something quite different". Famous examples from the distant past are Solomon's riddle for honey he discovered in the carcase of a lion:

Out of the eater came forth meat, and out of the strong came
forth sweetness.

and the riddle of the Sphinx:

What animal walks on four legs in the morning, two at noon,
and three in the evening?

Here are some modern examples:

What wears shoes, yet has no feet?
Whose income comes from simple interest?

What work by an artist could nobody else have created?

Each of these can readily be transformed into a crossword clue, thus:

It wears shoes, yet has no feet (8)
His income comes from simple interest (9)
Work of art nobody else could have created (4-8)

Conversely, one can imagine that there might have existed a riddle:

What cylinder is always jammed?

to inspire the justly famous *Times* clue (attributed to Adrian Bell):

This cylinder is jammed (5,4)

In such a clue, nothing but a definition is offered the solver, but that definition itself contains the cryptic element. Cryptic definitions, thus, constitute one exception to the general rule that a clue has two parts. Here are some further examples:

They tend to bring up unrelated issues (6-7)
Player trying to win a hand (9)
It's not hard to attract business (4,4)

In the United States, standard daily crosswords continue to have clues that are mainly definitional. Setters there, nevertheless, manage to show considerable ingenuity in devising definitions that are fair but misleading. My favourite example is:

Rake over the coals (3,4,2,4)

Here are some other examples:
Body image (6)
Northern hemisphere (5)
Jam ingredients? (4)

Weather report (7)
World record (5)

Further discussion and examples of cryptic definitions will be found in Chapter 4.

PLAYING WITH WORD MEANINGS

The English language is full of words that exhibit polysemy. Take "race" for example, which receives the following treatment in *Collins English Dictionary*:

race[1] (reɪs) *n* **1** a contest of speed, as in running, swimming, driving, riding, etc. **2** any competition or rivalry: *the race for the White House.* **3** rapid or constant onward movement: *the race of time.* **4** a rapid current of water, esp. one through a narrow channel that has a tidal range greater at one end than the other. **5** a channel of a stream, esp. one for conducting water to or from a water wheel or other device for utilizing its energy: *a mill race.* **6a** a channel or groove that contains ball bearings or roller bearings or that restrains a sliding component. **6b** the inner or outer cylindrical ring in a ball bearing or roller bearing. **7** *Austral. and N.Z.* a narrow passage or enclosure in a sheep yard through which sheep pass individually, as to a sheep dip. **8** *Austral.* a wire tunnel through which footballers pass from the changing room onto a football field. **9** *N.Z.* a line of containers coupled together, used in mining to transport coal. **10** another name for **slipstream** (sense 1). **11** *Archaic.* the span or course of life. **12 not in the race.** *Austral. informal.* given or having no chance. ◆ *vb* **13** to engage in a contest of speed with (another). **14** to engage (oneself or one's representative) in a race, esp. as a profession or pastime: *to race pigeons.* **15** to move or go as fast as possible. **16** to run (an engine, shaft, propeller, etc.) or (of an engine, shaft, propeller, etc.) to run at high speed, esp. after reduction of the load or resistance. ◆ See also **race off, races.**   [C13: from Old Norse *rās* running; related to Old English *rǣs* attack]
race[2] (reɪs) *n* **1** a group of people of common ancestry, distinguished from others by physical characteristics, such as hair type, colour of eyes and skin, stature, etc. Principal races are Caucasoid, Mongoloid, and Negroid. **2 the human race.** human beings collectively. **3** a group of animals or plants having common characteristics that distinguish them from other members of the same species, usually forming a geographically isolated group; subspecies. **4** a group of people sharing the same interests, characteristics, etc.: *the race of authors.*   [C16: from French, from Italian *razza*, of uncertain origin]
race[3] (reɪs) *n* a ginger root.   [C15: from Old French *rais*, from Latin *rādīx* a root]

Note the different levels of differentiation. The numbering as race[1], race[2], race[3] reflects distinct etymologies. The first derivation is from an Old Norse word meaning "running", giving the literal meaning of a running competition. As is typical of English, and language in general, the core literal meaning has become metaphorically extended to a competition of any sort, any form of rapid onward movement (eg, "the race of time"), the span of one's life, and so on.

The second distinct meaning is of a group of people or animals, whether biologically or culturally defined. The meaning can be further stretched, as in Burns's eulogy to the haggis "Great chieftain o' the puddin'-race!". And there is yet a third distinct meaning.

"Buff" is a word that I find particularly fascinating because of the multi-chained link between its contemporary meaning of "an enthusiast" and its origin in the Late Latin word "bufalus" meaning "buffalo". Buff is leather made from the skins of buffalo, and, by extension, the colour of that leather. In the 20th century, volunteer firemen in New York wore buff-coloured uniforms. People whose hobby was watching fires became known as "buffs", and the usage generalised to enthusiasts for any hobby.

It is also characteristic of English that it is often extended by taking a word that originally has a meaning as one part of speech and giving it a related meaning for another part of speech. This process has been accelerated in recent times by the Americans, who are notorious for turning nouns into verbs such as "to garage", "to bus", "to author"; in short, they are said to work on the principle that any noun can be verbed.

One type of riddle is based on double meanings, such as the following:

Which of the reptiles is a mathematician?

This riddle can be easily transformed into a crossword clue:

Reptilian mathematician (5)

This clue is an example of the "double definition" type, conforming to the two-part structure in the special sense that one component is a definition, and so is the other.

With respect to the above clue, note that whereas, in reading the clue, it is natural to interpret "reptilian" as an adjective, the word can also be a noun (a less common synonym for "reptile"). Thus the task set by the clue is to find a word that can mean either "a reptile" or "a mathematician".

Another way in which ambiguity can be exploited in double definition clues is illustrated by:

Weed cut (4)

Here it is natural, in reading the clue, to interpret "cut" as the past participle form of the verb, but as a second definition of the answer it must be interpreted as the present tense. "Hit", "set", and "put" are other verbs that afford this type of ambiguity, often useful to the setter.

PLAYING WITH WORD FRAGMENTS

By contrast with the foregoing, other types of traditional puzzles break up words and manipulate the fragments. Charades, in particular, have a long history, dating back to 1711 at least, according to *The Oxford Guide to Word Games*. The basic charade breaks a word into two or more parts, and presents clues for each part and for the whole. These puzzles were acted out at house parties or published, often in rhyming form:

My first means the same
As what's usually done
My second's a name
In short, for a son

My whole is whence came
A king, number one

Here is a classic example:

My first is a colour, my second a workman's instrument, and my whole a pretty little bird.

Such a construction is easily adapted as a crossword clue of a common type, the structure of which would be:

Definition of "yellow" + definition of "hammer" + definition of "yellowhammer"

(though the convention of cluing "the whole" last is not necessary). A possible clue along these lines (diverging from the original charade in order to read more naturally) is:

Chicken hit another bird (12)

(note the part-of-speech ambiguity of "chicken" which is taken as a noun to make sense of the clue, but as an adjective to derive the answer).

Here is a riddle that works along the same lines:

What Spanish instrument's familiar name
And fisher's occupation are the same?

Adapted as a crossword clue it might become:

What a fisherman has to do to get a Spanish instrument (8)

By contrast, here is a (very fine) riddle that requires subtraction of one part from the whole rather than addition of parts to create the whole:

From what can you take the whole and still have some left?

Again, this is easily tranformed into a crossword clue (with the addition of a definition):

Take the whole from this and you'll still have some left – good! (9)

Another popular type of puzzle from the past is the rebus, a puzzle involving combinations of letters (to be added or deleted), pictures, and symbols (such as "&"). For example, you might be asked to identify a bird and shown a combination of the letter P, a sketch of paintings hanging on a wall, and the letter B crossed out beside a picture of a bridge. From these elements, the bird is constructed: P + ART + (B)RIDGE Another bird might be clued by drawings of a king, a fish and an ear, together with the letter A crossed out.

While the building blocks are words rather than pictures, there is a clear relationship between such traditional puzzles and crossword clues that rely on construction kits, adding and subtracting words and bits of words. The examples of rebuses just considered, with appropriate modifications, could be reformulated as crossword clues such as:

With quiet cunning, head off game bird (9)
Top man has to angle for attention, ignoring a bird (10)

A further type of puzzle involving word fracture is when a word is hidden as a succession of letters within one or more words (as, for example, when looking at a poster, I noticed that there is a demon in Claude Monet).

Puzzles based on this idea have a relatively short history. Dudeney, in *300 Best Word Puzzles*, provides a number of examples of what he terms "buried word" puzzles, including the following:

Find the names of eight English poets in these lines:

The sun is darting rays of gold
Upon the moor, enchanting spot;
Whose purpled heights, by Ronald loved,
Up open to his shepherd cot.
And sundry denizens of air
Are flying, aye, each to his nest;
And eager make at such an hour
All haste to reach the mansions blest.

PLAYING WITH LETTERS

Other forms of playing with a written language are at the level of its letters. In particular, anagrams have a very long history, going back at least as far as the Greeks. According to Howard Bergerson, in his book *Palindromes and Anagrams* (Dover, 1973), they were invented by the Greek poet Lycophron in 260 BC (but how do we know he had no precursors?). Throughout subsequent history, anagrams of names have been used for many purposes, including flattery and denigration, as pseudonyms, invested with cabbalistic significance – or simply for amusement. Louis XIII of France appointed a Royal Anagrammatist. Many further fascinating examples will be found in Bergerson's book and in *The Oxford Guide to Word Games*.

Many of the historical examples of anagrams were for names of people, the highest accomplishment being a phrase that aptly described the person. One of the best and most well-known is Lewis Carroll's for Florence Nightingale:

Flit on, cheering angel

A more modern example dates from the time of Premium Bonds when a device call "ERNIE" (acronym for Electronic Random Number Indicator Equipment) was used to select prize-winners, provoking the rueful comment: "Ne'er I!". There is an anecdote about a crossword solver too engrossed in his puzzle as the plane prepared to take off. A stewardess approached and firmly instructed him to "truss neatly to be safe" (find the anagram).

Anagrams entered crosswords very quickly, originally in minimal form, such as:

Gets near (anag.) (8)

(which has at least three possible answers) but developed into the fully-fledged anagram clue familiar today in which the existence of the anagram is indicated by an appropriate word or phrase in the clue rather than the blatant "anag.", and a definition of the answer is provided. For example:

Drive off as convertible gets near (8)

A special case of an anagram is what Barnard in *Anatomy of the Crossword* called an "anadrome", in which the letters of one word are written in reverse order to form another word (or phrase, as in the literary example of Dylan Thomas's village of Llareggub in *Under Milk Wood*). Henry Ernest Dudeney posed the following puzzles:

Reverse (that is, read backwards) a mechanical power and
    have a feast.
Reverse one who is diseased and have to resist.
Reverse an evil one and have resided.
Reverse a falsifier and have a banister.
Reverse a measure and have an opening.
Reverse a disposition and have a destiny.

Straightforward variations on these, using more convenient definitions, could produce reasonable clues, for example:

Repelled evil one and survived (5) [A]
Show dishonest person up and express anger (4) [D]

(Note that the appropriate ways in which to indicate reversal differ depending on whether the clue is across or down.)

PLAYING WITH SOUND

If my memory is correct, it was Miles Kington who suggested that the motto of the French Naval Academy might be "To the water – the hour has come", ie, "A l'eau – c'est l'heure" (try saying that aloud). Punning on the basis of ambiguity in the sound of words or groups of words has long been a form of wit. Against Dryden's description of puns as "the lowest and most grovelling from of wit" may be set Fowler's comment that "the assumption that puns are *per se* contemptible ... is a sign at once of sheepish docility and the desire to seem superior".

Wordplays based on the sound of words are old and varied:

Q. Why need you never starve in the desert?
A. Because of the sand which is there.

Apart from Shakespeare, literary examples include Thomas Hood's:

His death, which happen'd in his berth
At forty-odd befell
They went and told the sexton
And the sexton toll'd the bell

And Belloc's:

When I am dead, I hope it may be said
His sins were scarlet, but his books were read

A famous historical example occurred when Sir Charles Napier disobeyed orders and conquered the province of Sind in 1843. He announced the capture by the single-word message "Peccavi", Latin for "I have sinned".

The most common basis for cryptic clues based on puns is single-word homophones, in which English abounds. The standard form of this type of clue has three components, namely a definition of the answer, a definition of its homophone, and an indication of the homophony:

> *We hear a couple of scores played loudly (5)*
> *Confessed – audibly? Just so (5)*
> *Pleasant voyage announced for lots of sailors (5)*

A further variation exploits the sound of individual letters, as in the classic:

YY U R
YY U B
I C U R
YY 4 me.

and the much more strained:

AB, F U NE X?
S V F X
F U NE M?
S V F M
OK, L F M N X.

Similarly, individual letters may be indicated by homophony in a cryptic clue, often to indicate a part of the answer, more unusually the whole, as in:

> *Reportedly why you seize a Mexican plant (5)*

ELABORATIONS

In exemplifying the ancestry of cryptic clues in earlier forms of puzzles and wordplay, I have, at the same time, introduced the most standard types of clue. These types are elaborated on in later chapters, dealing in turn with clues based on definitions (Chapter 4), anagrams

(Chapter 5), hidden clues (Chapter 6), construction clues (Chapter 7), and clues using homophones (Chapter 8). The remaining chapters deal with hybrid clues that draw on a mixture of these and other devices (Chapter 9) and with clues that extend the repertoire (Chapter 10).

PLAYING FAIR

A succinct statement of the principles of "square dealing" was made by Don Putnam in *Games and Puzzles*, a fine magazine that appeared in the 1970s, as follows:

1 Each clue should be a battle of wits, not a test of knowledge.

2 Each clue must contain a reference to the whole diagram word.

3 Each clue must also contain a gimmick (anagram, reversal, pun, etc, an indication of which must be subtly but fairly worked into the wording of the clue.

4 Each clue must be worded to make some sort of sense (preferably a misleading sense) in its own right, but …

5 The grammatical accuracy of the wording of the clue must not be sacrificed to this end.

As will be seen in the next chapter, these principles were by no means always adhered to in *The Times* crosswords during the earlier period of its evolution. However, they are now consistently followed, with the exception of the second part of the first principle stated. *Times* solvers are expected to have access to broad (but not too broad) cultural knowledge.

As stated in Putnam's second principle, a *sine qua non* of a fair clue is a definition that is sufficiently precise (see Chapter 4 for discussion of what constitutes a fair definition). The definition may strongly suggest a particular interpretation that sends the solver in the wrong direction while being perfectly adequate if interpreted appropriately. Indeed, a large part of the setter's ingenuity is devoted to achieving such effects.

With regard to the third principle of "Square Dealing", the typical cryptic clue has two components that are juxtaposed (in either order), one being a definition and the other a secondary indication of the answer that may take many forms. One exception to this rule, illustrated earlier in this chapter, is the cryptic definition clue, whereby the solver is presented with a definition only, the cryptic element being inherent in the definition. A second exception is the special case where the definition and secondary indication are not juxtaposed but coincide. This type of clue is called "& lit." since the clue can be read first as a cryptic indication of the answer, and then literally as a definition. A simple example is:

It can be reshuffled (7)

The final exception to the bipartite construction is that occasionally a clue offers a bonus in the form of an extra definition or an extra secondary indication.

The requirement that a clue make sense I have always taken very seriously. It is not unknown in crosswords appearing in other publications to find clues like:

Less hairy run is a lot of nonsense (10)

in which the clue, as well as the answer, is BALDERDASH. As succinctly put by my predecessor as editor, John Grant: "The most damning thing one can say about a crossword clue is that it could only be a crossword clue."

Another fundamental rule is that words should not be gratuitously inserted if they cannot be justified in terms of the structure of the clue. Unwarranted little words, in particular, tend to creep in. For example, there is no justification for "by" in:

Rents made ridiculous by people in business (9)

However, an appropriate word joining the two parts of the clue is fine:

Rents made ridiculous for people in business (9)

Commonly used joining words include "in", "as", "for", "from". Note that the first pair are bidirectional, by which I mean that the definition and the secondary indication that they link may come in either order. By constrast, "for" and "from" should only be used in one direction, thus:

[Secondary indication] for [definition]
[Definition] from [secondary indication]

Also, it is permissible, and often extremely convenient, to use "filler" or "neutral" words. For example, in the clue:

Bloomer made by reflective youth (9)

"made by" is useful to help the clue read sensibly, and indicates that the word indicated by the first definition is also generated by the second definition. In the following clue, "appears" is helpful to make the clue meaningful, and simply indicates that IT is part of the answer:

Not much accommodation available in county, it appears (6)

As well as making sense, the clue should be grammatically correct, of course, both as a phrase or sentence, and in terms of its construction as a clue. This point was exemplified in Chapter 1 in relation to Alec Robins's analysis of the flawed clue for PLAIN:

I am included in the plan, it's obvious (5)

Further, it is nowadays considered obligatory that the definition part of the clue should indicate the correct part of speech, a standard not always met in earlier crosswords. For example, the first *Times* Crossword includes as a clue for DIFFIDENT:

Wants confidence (9)

which clue unfairly (by today's standards) implies that the answer is a verb, rather than an adjective.

A further desideratum is that only one answer should fit the clue. While a well constructed cryptic clue will usually meet this criterion, it is always possible to overlook an alternative answer that fits the clue equally well, if not better. A simple example is the following:

Two little boys like the king (5)

The answer intended may be REGAL, but ROYAL fits just as well. (Note that "little" is a hint that the boys' names are short ones.) Double definition clues are most susceptible to this flaw. For example, there are (at least) two reasonable answers for:

Island drink (7)

In most cases, the harm can be undone, since the ambiguity will be settled by intersecting words, but the solver who has entered a wrong answer (particularly if one of those confident individuals who uses a pen) may be justifiably annoyed. Occasionally, if the setter is not alert, even the checking of letters will not help. If you are faced with _E_ON and the clue:

Fruit found on elm, oddly (5)

you may as well toss a coin to decide the answer. For the same reason, the careful setter avoids a clue such as:

Damage museum with falsehoods, we hear (9)

particularly if the penultimate letter is not checked, since the solver has no way of knowing if the answer should be spelt –IZE or –ISE.

Chapter 3
BECOMING
A TIMES SOLVER

EVOLUTION OF THE TIMES STYLE 1930–2001

The evolution of the *Times* style can conveniently be traced in *The Penguin Book of The Times 50th Anniversary Crosswords* (Penguin, 1980). This collection consists of one puzzle from February of each year, from the first puzzle of 1930 to a special Anniversary crossword published fifty years later. Both, as mentioned in Chapter 1, were composed by Adrian Bell.

In the first crossword created specifically for *The Times*, reproduced overleaf, the numbers of letters in the solutions were not provided at the ends of the clues, an elementary form of courtesy to the solver that was not introduced until some years later (and is still lacking in American crosswords).

The majority of the clues are definitional, ranging from "straight" definitions, such as 1 across and 3 down, to definitions that have a degree of crypticity, such as 23 across and 31 down. However, there are a substantial number of clues already exemplifying a range of cryptic devices. Several (eg, 42 down) provide two unrelated definitions. While two unadorned anagrams, unambiguously signalled by "anag.", are included, there is also a couple of fully-fledged anagrams (36 across and 50 across – note that the latter first requires "welcome" to be transformed into "greet"). 10 across exemplifies the combination of a definition and an alternative route to the answer through juxtaposing two parts separately defined, and 51 across is based on the reversal of one word to form another. 15 across exploits homophones, as indicated by "to speak".

1930 Crossword: Crossword Puzzle No.1

ACROSS

1 Spread unevenly
4 Part of a Milton title
10 A month, nothing more, in Ireland
11 He won't settle down
13 22 down should be this
15 Cotton onto, so to speak
17 Head of a chapter
18 Denizen of the ultimate ditch
21 Frequently under observation
23 What's in this stands out
25 Flighty word
26 If the end of this gets in the way the whole might result
27 Retunes (anag.)
30 This means study
33 Simply enormous
36 There's a lot in this voice
38 This elephant has lost his head
39 A turn for the worse
41 Done with a coarse file
43 Red loam (anag.)
45 This rodent's going back
47 Makes a plaything with its past
48 Wants confidence
50 A mixed welcome means getting the bird
51 This girl seems to be eating backwards
52 The men in the moon
53 A pinch of sand will make it dry

DOWN

2 Heraldic gold between mother and me
3 Out of countenance
4 Upset this value and get a sharp reproof
5 Intently watched
6 In some hands the things become trumpets
7 A religious service
8 This horseman has dropped an h
9 Sounds like a curious song
12 This ought to be square
14 Momentary stoppage
16 Written briefly
18 Calverley's picturesque scholars carved their names on every one
19 Site of 45 across
20 Precedes advantage
22 Parents in a negative way
24 Used to be somewhere in France
28 Happen afterwards
29 Climbing instinct in man
31 A terrestrial glider
32 The final crack
33 The little devil's on our money
34 Simplest creature
35 Time measurements
36 Jollier than 4 across
37 Ladies in promising mood
38 Presents are commonly this
40 Gets the boot
42 Hail in Scotland may mean tears
44 Works, but usually plays
46 She's dead
49 Only a contortionist could do this on a chair

By contrast with today's cryptics, in which it is accepted as a *sine qua non* that the clue contains a definition of the answer, there are several clues that give a cryptic indication of the answer without benefit of definition (38, 45, 47, 53 across, 2, 9, 49 down). Of these, 47 across is the most subtle ("see" plus its past "saw" = "seesaw").

4 across and 36 down refer to Milton's paired poems "Il Penseroso" (meaning "the contemplative man" – in fact, the correct Italian is "Penserioso") and "L'Allegro" ("the cheerful man"). Consulting *Brewer's Dictionary of Phrase and Fable* explains the answer to 46 down; "Queen Anne is dead" is defined therein as "A slighting retort made to a teller of stale news". The quotation from Calverley used as the basis of 18 down is from *Gemini and Virgo* (not included in the *Oxford Dictionary of Quotations*).

1940 Crossword

ACROSS	DOWN
4 It used to be a bathing costume (8)	**1** Barkis was (7)
9 'I have been faithful to thee, Cynara! In my __' (Dowson) (7)	**2** The more confused (7)
10 Paradoxically, the clock is still working when this (two words) (2,6)	**3** A stirring game (5)
11 The legal official has become or turned a singer (7)	**5** It goes up and down with lights (two words) (6,4)
12 Surely of meaning to you (8)	**6** Dynamic nationalities? (two words) (5,5)
13 The number of kings of Essex (5)	**7** A slangy drink in a French one (5)
17 Mule tours make one shaky (9)	**8** The one cricketer who is always out (two words) (7,3)
18 A hit to embarrass (5)	**13** A condition powder might be wrapped in this (two words) (5,5)
20 The Emperor gives us the bird (5)	**14** It is a very near thing for most of us (4)
21 This Shakespearian has the devil in her (9)	**15** Rinse Dumas (anag.) (10)
24 A lady known to Jane Austenites (5)	**16** Pioneer of the round cruise (two words) (6,4)
25 A misleading implication, they really transport men (8)	**19** A most curtailed fellow (4)
28 Free, or empty (two words) (4,3)	**22** Architectural feature in Cornwall (7)
29 Patrick's girl (8)	**23** 'He does it with better grace, but I do it more __' (Shakespeare) (7)
30 Where Lancelot changed shields (7)	**26** Town with go-ahead trade, so to speak (5)
31 Conceit of the engaged? (8)	**27** Make a donkey into a poet (5)

In the next puzzle, from ten years later, the most obvious development is that almost all the clues are cryptic in one way or another. One exception is the inclusion of two direct quotation clues (9 across, 23 down). There are several other literary references, that in 24 across being to *Lady Susan,* an unpublished work of Jane Austen. The clue for 1 down is subtly misleading, and no doubt very many solvers wrote in WILLING, since "Barkis is willing" is such a familiar quotation from *David Copperfield.*

The unadorned anagram, without definition, is still there (15 down). Other anagrams lack a definition (2 down) or anagram indicator (12, 17 across). Several other clues are also without benefit

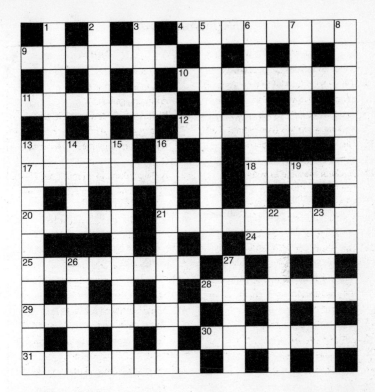

of definition, in particular the whimsical concoctions 31 across and 6 down. Other clues run the gamut of more or less complex constructions (for example, 11 across), double definition clues (for example, 28 across) and a homophonic clue (26 down, though the connection between "loot" and "trade" is not clear to me).

Next consider the 1950 representative (overleaf). There are four quotation clues, including two from poets of whom I must confess I have not heard. It was still acceptable to offer cryptic clues lacking a definition of the answer, 8 across (the reference is to *Evan Harrington* by Meredith) and 2 down being clear examples. Anagrams of the blatant "anag." type were still common at this time, as well as anagram clues in which an anagram is not, as is the usual practice today, indicated in some way (for example, 1 across).

1950 Crossword

ACROSS	DOWN

ACROSS

1 I call for the colour of a sun-bonnet (5)

4 A sequence of letters? (5-4)

8 Harrington puts the low-down first (7)

9 The smithy shade lacks a large box (3-4)

10 This screw isn't double income (4)

11 It gets a licking (5)

12 'Quoted __, and jewels five-words long' (Tennyson) (4)

15 See the new girl (anag.) (8-5)

17 Cycling coppers: the first four times as good as the second (5-8)

20 Insular turn for a seaman (4)

21 A bit of the course that must be put back (5)

22 '__ die' (4)

25 '__ my boy, my boy, sessa! Let him trot by' (*King Lear*) (7)

26 College street (7)

27 A day for football in Yorkshire (9)

28 Explosive sculpture (5)

DOWN

1 She is not, necessarily, one of small tonnage (9)

2 Turned over French bed in a French town (7)

3 Beware this man! (4)

4 No stern action (anag.) (13)

5 Fruit of controversy (4)

6 Shorten with a structure (7)

7 Welsh national wear (5)

9 When there is the last rush for standing room (10,3)

13 Not quite room enough for a Yankee in the colony (5)

14 'A frugal __, Whose constant cares were to increase his store' (Home) (5)

16 Here one might have met Jane Austen (4,5)

18 Writing instrument dripped red ink? (7)

19 'The __ of our blood and state Are shadows, not substantial things' (Shirley) (7)

20 Marlow does so finish (5)

23 Perhaps it pinches so he changes it (4)

24 Rough fellow for washing (4)

There are several clues based on definitions of varying degrees of crypticity, of which I judge 9 down the best. Other clues recognisable as standard types include 17 across (definition plus build-up), 20 across (based on reversal), 26 across (two definitions), 23 down (definition plus anagram).

The grid construction could be considered somewhat lazy, with no fewer than eight answers having more unchecked letters than checked.

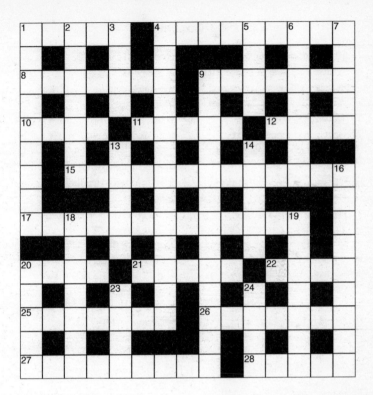

22 across is more reminiscent of an American puzzle, in which the odd-looking answer OFA, for example, can be accommodated by a clue such as "Son __ gun". It is distinctly odd, moreover, since the answer is signalled as a four-letter word, yet there is no definition or any other indication of that word in the clue.

In the 1965 puzzle (overleaf), apart from one direct quotation clue, 11 across relates to characters in Thackeray's *Vanity Fair*, and 2 down combines references to *The Amateur Gentleman* by John Jeffrey Farnol, and *The Amateur Poacher* by Richard Jefferies (does one detect here the pen of Adrian Bell, like Jefferies a chronicler of rural England?).

Anagram indicators still were not *de rigueur*, apparently (22 down)

1965 Crossword

ACROSS	DOWN
1 What Shakespeare wrote with? It put rather a restraint on his first acts, surely (4-3)	**1** Pod (3-6)
5 A sound measure (7)	**2** Farnol's Gentleman, Jefferies's Poacher (7)
9 Of help in covering up? (5)	**3** Straw for the friendly donkey? (9)
10 A dog on foot belonging to us, Madame (9)	**4** Drinks for when the frost is sharp (4)
11 One had a faithful Dobbin (6)	**5** Crane to see a girl (10)
12 Does it make a hole in the pocket – just a little one? (3-5)	**6** Attractive trinket (5)
14 People with whom Miss Muffet got spoony? (5)	**7** Been longer in the sun? (7)
15 Concerted initiatives (9)	**8** Transport from Redhill or Rye (5)
18 What one has suffered on the one-fifty, Flora! (9)	**13** The way is first left, then right, it's quite a long walk (5,5)
20 Strains of harvest home (5)	**16** It's simply disgraceful! (9)
22 Bound to be uppish (4,4)	**17** Gravity hindered this task (9)
24 First-rate vantage point (6)	**19** A 13 would have been quite the usual thing for him (7)
26 Astronomical figures (9)	**21** 'The soul's dark __, battered and decayed' (Waller) (7)
27 To you and me old-time means practice (5)	**22** What a shame to hang round Dobbin's neck! (5)
28 What we do on waking, to some extent (7)	**23** Resort for a square meal? (5)
29 Has the lady been in for a drink? (7)	**25** Jobs not begun – why? (4)

and clues with only whimsical definitions still acceptable (1 down). No fewer than three clues exploit homophones without signalling this feature (9, 14 across, 3 down). There are many double definition clues (20, 28 across, 4, 5, 6, 19 down). The first hidden clue in our small sample makes its appearance at 8 down.

Apart from 1 down, each clue does have a definition, but in many cases, there is still a loose fit between the part of speech of the answer and that suggested by the clue. For example, in 25 down there is no indication that the answer is a verb. In other cases, such as 29 across, the definition is decidedly elliptical.

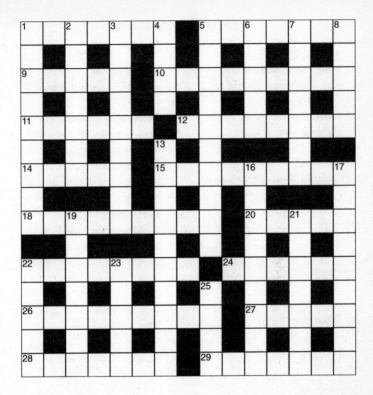

The 1980 puzzle (overleaf) brings us to the golden jubilee of *The Times* Crossword, celebrated by the publication on 1 February of an appropriately auriferous offering by Adrian Bell. On the occasion of its publication, Philip Howard wrote in celebration that "Number 1 was published on 1 February 1930, having been compiled by a young man called Adrian Bell, who had never solved a crossword before, let alone set one. Adrian Bell, the elder statesman of letters and king of crosswords, compiled the golden jubilee puzzle … as gilded with references to that old *Au* as if Midas had been handling his quill pen". Adrian Bell's reaction, on discovering that he was included in *The Guinness Book of Records* as "Most Durable Compiler" was to wonder whether that achievement would get him to heaven or hell. "Think of the time wasted," he wrote, "while company directors,

1980 Crossword

ACROSS	DOWN

ACROSS

1 Never a cross word in 1887 (6,7)

9 Lay of Midas's ocarina? Or of one of 1 down (6,3)

10 A once gold coin I love in Latin American locality (5)

11 Alloy as might be attached to a sovereign (5)

12 Inscribed 'I promise to pay' back – for its school fees? (4)

13 Gustave the golden (4)

15 To wit his written work gives us the splits (7)

17 A glistering performance on the breakers is not necessarily golden (7)

18 Nut of the jeunesse dorée (7)

20 Maybe a 9 to attract more, if one doesn't cut the cackle (4-3)

21 Not the Golden Rose, but a different sort, love (4)

22 The this, said Hamlet, is a golden quantity (4)

23 A Thomas (trigger-happy?) in odd company (5)

26 Character of wood, hoof and horn (5)

27 The Golden Treasury, by Burlington House musicians (9)

28 Straitway into heaven for US, St Francis? (3,6,4)

DOWN

1 Lots of silly females, though one could make a valuable deposition (7,2,5)

2 £3, nothing in that and short of yen, for suckers (5)

3 Synonymously gilt-edged perhaps, to be a sight better off (3-7)

4 They express no golden opinions (7)

5 Pope's gold one gone missing among the flora? (7)

6 If gold is it likely to fall? (4)

7 Eruptive isle of exile of 20-franc gold piece, so to speak at length (9)

8 Eg, Britain on the gold standard? (9,5)

14 Shelled wreck of a sun-car, etc. (10)

16 Apparatus of golden reflections (9)

19 Not 'my bow of burning gold' in *Jerusalem*, just the quiver (7)

20 Unfestive cake, it's observed (7)

24 Looking-glass messenger from Manhattan (5)

25 A lustrous prize to tempt Selima (4)

stockbrokers, bankers, civil servants, concentrate on that last word in *The Times* Crossword which they failed to solve in the train coming up."

By the time of the 1980 crossword, the current style of *The Times* Crossword had very largely become established. While maintaining the wit of earlier decades, the technical soundness of clues had been

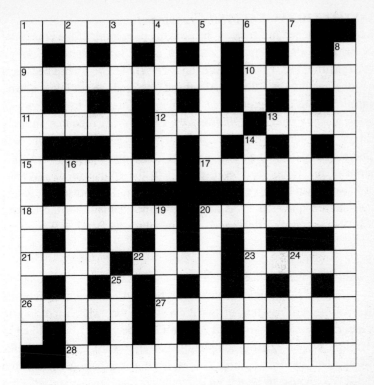

tightened up considerably. For the Golden Jubilee puzzle, in the cause of ingeniously linking most clues to the theme, a few are perhaps more oblique than might be considered strictly reasonable. For example, two preliminary shifts are necessary when solving 7 down to identify ELBA as the object of anagrammatisation.

The reference in 1 across is, of course, to an earlier Golden Jubilee, namely that of Queen Victoria. There is a sprinkling of literary references, including (obliquely) Hamlet's last words "The rest is silence" (22 across), Selima, the tragic heroine of Gray's *Ode on the Death of a Favourite Cat Drowned in a Tub of Gold Fishes* (25 down) and Pope's description of Lord Hervey as a "bug with gilded wings" (5 down).

INSTITUTIONALISATION

As had happened in America, the growing popularity of the crossword in Britain soon generated a range of social manifestations (Arnot, 1981; Millington, 1974). Before long, *The Times* Crossword became a national institution. Edmund Akenhead (my predecessor but one, who enrolled me as an apprentice in 1975), in his foreword to *The Penguin Book of The Times 50th Anniversary Crosswords*, recounts an early tribute of a kind, when, on 24 September 1934, a defendant was charged with "damaging a copy of *The Times* displayed in the reading room of the Battersea Free Library". In the course of 22 days the crossword had been cut out of the paper on 18 occasions. To the magistrate's question "Was any other paper damaged?" the answer was "No, sir, only *The Times*". The penalty was fixed at 9 shillings with 21 shillings costs.

Much of the lore associated with *The Times* Crossword concerns fast solution times, real or imagined, boasted or envied. Surely the best-known story is that of the Provost of Eton, who, according to a letter to *The Times* from Sir Austen Chamberlain in 1934, liked to time his boiled egg by completing the crossword, and didn't like his egg hard-boiled. Among the reactions was a famous letter from P. G. Wodehouse in which he commented that "To a man who has been beating his head against a wall for 20 minutes over a single anagram it is g. and wormwood to read a statement like that one about the Provost of Eton and the eggs." Another correspondent wrote as follows:

I had hoped from Sir Austen's letter that boiling an egg might
Help. I started at 8.00 and it is now 15.05 and I am still wondering
Who is the uncle of Israel, and the egg has burst.

At the risk of being vilified as a spoiler of a good myth, I must report that a correspondent from Eton informed me that the famous Provost was "a keen but inexpert solver, often still baffled by a clue or two at dinner-time". A letter to *The Times* in 1962 stated that the then crossword editor, Jane Carton, had shown that it was not physically possible to read out the clues and fill in the answers in less than four or five minutes.

However, plausible though it sounds, this claim has been disproved under carefully controlled conditions. The official world record is held by Roy Dean who tells the story thus:

> One morning … my train was late and I had to spend a little
> time in the station waiting room. I turned to the crossword …
> began to fill it in, and realised that I had solved it in the $4^1/2$
> minutes before the train arrived. This prompted me to write to
> the editor of *The Times* suggesting that, as the *Guinness Book
> of Records* already contained an entry for the slowest solution
> of the crossword (spread over 34 years), it might be a good
> idea to have the fastest one. My letter appeared in the paper
> on Saturday, 19 December, 1970.

> I was woken up at 6 o'clock … It was the *Today* programme
> on BBC's Radio 4. The presenter had seen my letter in
> *The Times* and asked me to come to the studio … for an
> interview … In the studio I was told that they would like me
> to have a go at that day's crossword … with a view to setting
> up a record. I agreed, with some trepidation, and started the
> puzzle against the stopwatch. I was incredibly lucky; although
> the Saturday crossword was usually the most difficult of the
> week, the puzzles had somehow got out of order and the one I
> had to solve would have been Monday's, which was quite
> straightforward. When I put my pen down the stopwatch said
> 3 minutes and 45 seconds.

Since the establishment of this official record, there have been at least two plausible claims to have beaten this record, by Paul Henderson and John Henderson (not related), but these feats have not been officially ratified.

In the annual *Times* Crossword Championship (currently

sponsored by WordCross, the Internet crossword site), solvers compete against each other to solve four crosswords as quickly as possible. In regional heats, and subsequently in the national final, they complete four puzzles, with the winners typically averaging less than ten minutes per puzzle.

On the other hand, most solvers are happy to spend considerably more time, as expressed in verse in 1976 by Mr James Elliott (quoted by Edmund Akenhead in the aforementioned preface):

> Sir
> I cannot guess how many puzzles
> In a year
> You may assemble
> But humble
> As a part-time addict wish to thank
> You for an hour of pleasure
> Each weekday morning on the train
> Lunchtime in a pub
> And dreaming in between
>
> Your competition season
> Starts again
> But speaking simply for myself
> I deem half done a pass
> And once a week completion
> Rare success
>
> If ever
> But it's most unlikely
> The Puzzle solves me in ten minutes
> I shall take up embroidery
> Or knitting
> And muse to the needle click
> Of happier times

So thank you sir for this engendering
Of hours of gentle cogitation
Dulcet pleasures
Quite innocent of agitation
A puzzle
With no competition

Ability to solve *The Times* Crossword has become a symbol of high intelligence. In *The Strange World of the Crossword*, Roger Millington related how this particular expertise was cited in court as a measure of intellect (another instance of the curious affinity between crosswords and the law). The other side in the case, however, pointed out that "there are very stupid people who can do it easily and professors of the Royal Society who cannot do it at all".

There is a long-standing relationship between crosswords and another form of intelligence, going back to the famous story of the D-Day code words that turned up in *The Daily Telegraph* Crossword, and the feats of the crackers of the Enigma codes at Bletchley Park, many of whom were crossword experts. More recently, Peter Wright in *Spycatcher* affirmed that almost all the senior officers at MI5 spent the first half hour of the day on *The Times* Crossword. However, his account includes a strange reference to "seven down in the bottom left-hand corner" which, if you think about it, doesn't correspond to any normal design of a 15 × 15 grid, and certainly not any used in *The Times*.

Turning to what is certainly fictional, in John Le Carré's *Tinker, Tailor, Soldier, Spy*, the enduring sharpness of the mind of the ageing Connie Sachs when she is visited by Smiley in Oxford is succinctly conveyed as follows:

On the table lay a copy of the day's *Times*, crossword uppermost. Each square was inked in laboured letters. There were no blanks.

Colin Dexter's Inspector Morse is another fictional character whose intellectual brilliance is manifested by his ability to solve crosswords as well as murder puzzles from cryptic clues. Here, for example is how he begins a journey from Oxford in *The Wench is Dead*:

He bought *The Times* and the *Oxford Times* at the bookstall, got a seat at the back of the train, and had solved *The Times* crossword by Didcot. Except for one clue.

… He quickly wrote in a couple of bogus letters (in case any of his fellow-passengers were waiting to be impressed).

TIMES CROSSWORD STYLE AND CONVENTIONS

Beyond the general principles of fair cluing set out in Chapter 2, which are generally shared by comparable crosswords in other publications, *The Times* Crossword conforms to a number of specific guidelines and conventions in regard to the construction of both the grids and the clues.

By the time I became a member of the contributing team in 1976, many of the current guidelines had been established. There was a fixed set of 25 grids, and shortly after taking over as editor, I introduced 25 more. All of these grids satisfy the criteria that at least 50 per cent of the letters in any answer are checked (occur at the intersection of across and down entries) and that no more than two letters in succession are unchecked.

Accordingly, there is an inaccuracy in the Inspector Morse tale *The Inside Story* which appears in the collection of short stories *Morse's Greatest Mystery*, in which Morse is supposedly faced with _E_S_I_ as the last clue to solve in a *Times* crossword:

Jerry-built semi is beginning to collapse in such an upheaval (7)

Some of the guidelines that the team of *Times* setters are expected to respect are the following:

- no more than five complete anagrams in any puzzle
- at most one hidden clue
- no references to living people (with the sole exception of ER for the monarch)
- no inclusion of potentially upsetting words such as names of serious illnesses, offensive or derogatory terms
- avoidance of more than three plurals ending in S and minimal repetition of common prefixes and suffixes such as OVER-, UN-, -ING, -ATION
- no obscure words (discussed below)

Among specific conventions are these:

- "one" in a clue may appear in an answer as I, but not A (this is very clearly a matter of convention and tradition, since "a" is a perfectly good synonym for "one")
- "on" in an across clue means following rather than preceding when used to indicate the juxtaposition of parts of the answer, as in:

Fastening that comes undone is a problem on undergarment (8)

- a number written as one or two digits in the clue refers to the clue of that number (with *ac* or *dn* added if necessary to distinguish between across and down clues with the same number). For example, given the answer to 8 down is SECOND IN COMMAND, the following is a possible clue:

This girl's 8, as it happens (5)

- "to" in the infinitive form of a verb within a clue may be ignored, as illustrated in this clue:

It's trendy to like old colour (6)

where "to like" is used to indicate "dig" – being strictly logical it should indicate "to dig".

THE SOLVER'S EQUIPMENT

What does the solver need to know to be able to complete most of *The Times* Crossword most of the time?

VOCABULARY

As far as vocabulary goes, obscure words are avoided. A high percentage of the vocabulary should be familiar to a person of a reasonable level of education and knowledge (what is reasonable, I refuse to attempt to define), mostly without recourse to reference books, while commuting to work on a train, for example. Thus words such as TAGHAIRM, defined in *Chambers* as "(in the Scottish Highlands) divination ; *esp* inspiration sought by lying in a bullock's hide behind a waterfall", will not appear.

On the other hand, one of the benefits of doing crosswords is learning new words, so an occasional less common word is justifiable. A good principle to follow is to compensate for a less familiar word by making the clue easy and the build-up such that the solver can be reasonably confident of having found the right answer even if the word remains to be checked in a dictionary later.

It is traditional in *The Times* Crossword to restrict words from foreign languages to a minimum of the most familiar. It would be restrictive, of course, to forbid setters to use the ever-so-convenient foreign articles indicated by "the Spanish", "a Parisian" and so on. Here is a selection of clues using common French words or French terms that have entered our language:

Weekend football, for example (9)
With nothing better to do, take a term of French (5,2,5)

How De Gaulle announced his resignation? (4,2,3)

Other languages that may be used occasionally in clues include American:

Aircraft controller's alternative to flights in US (8)
Metal I once extracted for Americans (8)

KNOWLEDGE BASE

The competent solver is assumed to have a wide, but not exhaustive, general knowledge. Not everyone can be Jowett, celebrated thus in *The Masque of Balliol* composed by members of the college in 1870:

> First come I; my name is Jowett.
> There's no knowledge but I know it.
> I am Master of this college:
> What I don't know isn't knowledge.

A worthy successor to Jowett was John Sykes (1929–93), who dominated *The Times* Crossword Championship, winning it ten times between its inception in 1970 and his retirement through ill-health after the 1990 event. He would certainly have won it more often if he had entered every year. His claim that his work as a lexicographer (editor of the *Concise Oxford Dictionary*) gave him what he called a "marginal advantage" is perhaps acceptable in the sense that the more fundamental reason for his superiority was intellectual brilliance. An indication of his polymathy in his obituary was the story of how, as a physicist attending a meeting with Russian scientists, finding that a key paper had not been translated into Russian, he produced his own translation overnight.

The judgment of what a person with a well-rounded education should know is inevitably subjective. Robert Norton, writing to my predecessor John Grant in 1984 suggested the following characterisation:

It has always, surely, been axiomatic that a reasonably well-stocked, if somewhat devious, mind is sufficient equipment to embark on this daily challenge. One needs to know the remnants of some Latin, the first verse of the "Destruction of Sennacherib" (?), some "Kubla Khan", quotations from *Hamlet*, *Macbeth* and one or two others, certainly stopping after *Henry the Fourth* Part Two, and not including Part One. Hardly any musical knowledge is needed, once one can spell words like minim and semibreve. But it is an advantage to know a little of the theatre ... and to have spent enough time playing soldiers to be able to distinguish between REME (for trireme) and RE, RAC and RM. Some cricket, the titles of a few musicals, and the stock is almost complete.

As editor, my subjective judgments were guided by decades of experience as a solver and, later, setter. Inevitably, these judgments were biased, to a degree, by my own intellectual background. I tended somewhat towards the pragmatic principle that something was obscure if I didn't know it, and conversely. In general, the principle is that a solver should not – too often – be left at a loss because of the obscurity of some piece of information. On the other hand, as with the enlargement of vocabulary, an important side-effect of solving crosswords is being made aware of previously unknown important, interesting, or amusing titbits through being sent off to comb through the pages of *The Oxford Dictionary of Quotations, Brewer's Dictionary of Phrase and Fable,* or whatever.

The deepest source of material for interesting clues is, of course, literature. Through the medium of a cryptic crossword, straight questions such as:

Who wrote about a detective called Father Brown?
Who wrote plays called *Uncle Vanya* and *Three Sisters*?

can be cryptically transformed thus:

Writer whose father was a detective (10)

He had an uncle and sisters on the stage (7)

Here is a further selection of other clues based on literature of varying degrees of familiarity:

Pampered, like the Owl and the Pussy-Cat? (5-3)
(included for nostalgic reasons, since it was the first clue in my first *Times* puzzle, published in 1976)
Nobody was, for example, like Evelyn (7)
Comedy that was written for a lark, originally (6,6)
Abridged history book by Waugh (7,3,4)
With initial revision, Milton's Paradise Lost *(7-2)*
Poetry making dreadful hardship so real (1,10,3)
Novel event in Pilgrim's Progress *(6,4)*
Rosy prospects here for City after half-time (5)
Medical assistant for famous consultant (6,6)
Part-time medic (6)
No man's land (6,4)

These are at the less familiar end of the spectrum, I would say:

A relative of Lear, connected in obscure way (9)
Letter from Israel included in March issue (4)
King he wrote about was Henry (6)

One type of literary clue that I decided to abandon, on taking over the editorship, was the quotation clue. One of the reasons for doing so was that it seemed illogical to retain a type of clue that does not have any cryptic character. As a solver, I thought such clues were either too easy (I knew the answer) or, more often, frustrating (I didn't know, and guessing, even if successful, was not satisfactory).

By contrast, I find clues indirectly or cryptically based on familiar quotations much more interesting. Here are some examples:

Block not part of Lovelace's prison (9)

A distant county, going by air (9)
Ruler of Queen's Navee was never so perplexed (2,3)
PM whose opponents never meet? (5)

and this one is especially subtle:

Tell Macduff to lead on to fresh fields and pastures new,
*   for example (8)*

Other indirect quotations relate to proverbial wisdom and common sayings:

Dog that delights shepherd (3,6)
Poet's unenforceable command to horse (10)
Going to fire from this vessel? That's even more dangerous (6-3)
No trouble, unlike Roman architecture (3,2,1,4,4)
Representative who shouldn't be narrow-minded? (9)

Having myself "small Latin and less Greek", the number of references to classical literature (though not, perhaps, mythology) decreased during my tenure. However one feels about it, the number of schoolchildren studying the classics is not what it was, and it is necessary to make some allowances for the up-and-coming generation of solvers. I do plead guilty to the following, however, which is in dubious taste, but irresistible:

In which three couples get together for sex (5)

As with literature, straight questions about music and art can be transformed into appropriately misleading cryptic clues. For example, most people know who wrote *The Four Seasons*, but might not immediately spot that this information is the basis of the clue:

He scored every season with great skill (7)

Some more examples:

Composer best known for magical pupil (5)
Hogarth's work not offered to Daisy (8,1,2,4)
Chaps sent in late to protect their betters, as depicted by
 Rembrandt (13)
Beauty a man with oils contrived (4,4)
Englishman who put together an astronomical score (5)
Prokofiev's beloved trio (7)

My limited knowledge of history and geography ensured that I did not emulate Macaulay, who, according to *The Oxford Companion to English Literature*, "was apt to attribute to schoolboys a range of historical and literary knowledge not usually found among them", as in "Every schoolboy knows who imprisoned Montezuma and who strangled Atahualpa". (Presumably, he did not expect schoolgirls to know anything.) Here are some examples of historical clues:

Neither Charles III nor Louis VI of France was so intelligent (8)
A Pope numbered as one having pride (7)
Anti-tax demonstration by apparently brave group (6,3,5)
Eastern capital invested once, making fortune today (7)
King with no followers in battle (6,3,6)
Former lover, by Elizabeth I beheaded (5)

The most obvious contribution of geography to crosswords is the group of three-letter rivers, Exe, Don, Dee, Cam, Ure, Tay, and so on, invaluable in the build-up of clues for many otherwise difficult-to-handle words. Examples of more substantive reference to geographical knowledge include:

One can't sink any lower than this (4,3)
State with sea to the East (5)
Part of the Empire once ruled by Victoria (7,8)
Country which has, North-East, China (5)

Sports and games have always featured prominently. Solvers are certainly expected to know the fielding positions and other terms connected with cricket. My own background predisposes me towards clues relating (at least ostensibly) to bridge and chess (which also offer convenient ways to deal with N, E, S, W and Q(ueen), K(ing), R(ook), B(ishop), (k)N(ight), P(awn) respectively):

> *Oddly East twice bid nothing – no trump is biddable (8)*
> *Repeatedly divulge information in one club, say (9)*
> *Ring with no diamonds, for example, resembling Faberge's work? (5)*
> *Information partners gathered about opponents (4)*
> *Learner winning at chess very quickly (7)*
> *Moved king to safety, escorted by company (7)*
> *Good opening – queen isn't taken by knight (7)*
> *The highest thing on board in the station (5,5)*
> *Bird cornered, unable to move at first (4)*

By comparison with other manifestations of culture, references to mathematics and science are relatively rare. While accepting that this inequity reflects the intellectual imbalance in our society I feel a degree of unease that it may also contribute to that imbalance. Be that as it may, solvers are not expected to know about calculus, topology, genetics, subatomic physics, the theory of relativity or the names of mathematicians and scientists beyond the most famous.

From a mathematical point of view, sin is a function (I refer, of course, to the companion of cos); however, I consistently disallowed "function" as a definition of SIN as part of an answer on the assumption that most readers would remember it only as the ratio associated with an angle in a right-angled triangle of opposite side over hypotenuse. Clues depending on mathematical knowledge tend to be restricted to elementary arithmetic, as in:

> *In which, when pairs are removed, one remains (7)*
> *Power of two oarsmen (5)*
> *Record total produced by working around the clock (7-5)*

or the most familiar of references:

Change to graph, say, for mathematician (10)

MOVING WITH THE TIMES

In considering what it is reasonable for the solver to be expected to know, it is important to be sensitive to the fact that solvers forty years younger than me are likely to be unaware of literature, music, radio and TV programmes, and other aspects of culture, that were prominent when I was their age. They listen to CDs and may well have never heard of an LP, let alone an EP. The risk of oldfogeyism is particularly high in the world of crosswords because crossword setters seem to be blessed with longevity and because crosswords themselves, like dictionaries, have an embalming effect on cultural knowledge, words and usages that otherwise have almost entirely disappeared from the current generation's consciousness.

In the realm of literature, do people still read John Buchan, A. J. Cronin, the Biggles books, the stories about Billy Bunter, the "William" books by Richmal Crompton? I may well be wrong, but my subjective judgment is that these works are dated. Winnie the Pooh is surely timeless, but can the same be said of Rupert Bear?

In the foreword to the *Sixteenth Book of The Times Crosswords* (Times Books, 1993), my predecessor, John Grant, wrote as follows:

Extra-terrestrial, surely, must go, useful though it was for
cluing words ending in –ET, before Stephen Spielberg's film
is quite forgotten. Similarly IT for SA, or sex-appeal,
popularised by the novelist Elinor Glyn in *It* (1927). It is
still in the dictionaries, but I cannot believe anyone has used
it thus since Word War II.

The other side of the coin is that new words enter the language, and old words change their meaning; this is the nature of language. Christopher Wren was delighted when King George commented that

St Paul's was "amusing, awful, and artificial" because at that time the words meant "amazing, awe-inspiring, and artistic". Words are coined for technical use or to describe social change, Americanisms and computerese enrich or corrupt our language depending on one's point of view, but there is no way to stop the language evolving.

REFERENCE BOOKS

The standard dictionaries on which *Times* setters rely are *Collins English Dictionary*, the *Concise Oxford*, and *Chambers Dictionary*. The first two are restricted to more or less familiar words, while the latter contains many more obscurities, and is the standard work for the really difficult crosswords such as those created by Azed and the *Listener* series. One will find in *Chambers* many idiosyncratic spellings of archaic words used by Spenser, Shakespeare, Milton, and so on, a plethora of Scotticisms, and many other words of extreme rarity.

Chambers is also notable in that it contains a number of humorous definitions, such as **ages**: a long time, however short; **he-man**: a man of exaggerated or extreme virility, or what some women consider to be virility; and, most famously **éclair**: a cake long in shape but short in duration. It cannot compare in this regard, of course, with the *Devil's Dictionary* by Ambrose Bierce, which defines "dictionary" itself as "A malevolent literary device for cramping the growth of a language and making it hard and inelastic" and "lexicographer" as "A pestilent fellow who, under the pretence of recording some particular stage in the development of a language, does what he can to arrest its growth, stiffen its flexibility and mechanize its method." This view is not true today, as there has been a marked swing in lexicographical principles from prescription (laying down how words should be used) towards description (reflecting how words are used) aided by large corpuses of language stored on computers.

Chambers is useful for checking definitions, but, for a word to be acceptable for use in *The Times* Crossword a good rule of thumb is that it should appear in the *Concise Oxford* and *Collins English Dictionary*, and preferably both. The latter is particularly useful in that it contains also proper nouns, such as names of major cities, rivers, people, and so on. The same applies to *The New Oxford Dictionary of English* (colloquially referred to as "Noddy") which is more comprehensive than the *Concise Oxford* and claims to contain "all those terms forming part of the enduring common knowledge of English speakers" (such as "Dolly Parton" and "Tammy Wynette").

A feature of dictionaries that has become clear to me over decades of thumbing through them is the surprising degree of inconsistency among them in terms of definitions, usage, and spellings. For example, a solver took issue with spelling the Hungarian dance as "czardas" rather than "csardas". *Collins* gives only the former spelling, the *Concise Oxford* includes the former as a variant of the latter, and *Chambers* states that the former is an erroneous spelling. "Entremets" is defined in *Chambers* as "a light dish served at table between the main courses" and the definition in the *Concise Oxford* is almost identical, but the first meaning given for it in *Collins* is "a dessert".

Apart from dictionaries, there are several reference works that are particularly useful for the solver who does not have the requisite knowledge in her or his head. As a basic set, I would suggest *Brewer's Dictionary of Phrase and Fable*, *The Oxford Companion to English Literature*, *The Penguin Dictionary of Proper Names*, and a dictionary of fictional characters (not so easy to find – mine is a rather elderly *Everyman's*). Other works that are of more use to the setter than the solver include thesauri (as well as Roget's classic, I find *Collins English Thesaurus* very useful) and *Chambers Biographical Dictionary*.

Another lesson I have learned over the years, particularly during my time as editor, is that the most highly-regarded of reference works cannot be assumed to be free of error. The most painful experience occurred when I was setting a Jumbo Crossword and, on the authority of one such reference, included, reading downwards through the puzzle, A CHILD'S GARDEN OF VERSE which I took to be a work by Robert Louis Stevenson. When I discovered at the last moment that it should be VERSES rather than VERSE it took several hours to repair the damage. Edmund Akenhead's advice was to check everything, and the more sure you are of something (his example was the assumption that the first name of the former Prime Minister Wilson was Harold), the more important it is to check. (Wilson's first name was James.)

Chapter 4

BY DEFINITION

With the evolution of the crossword clue from pure and simple definition, a variety of cryptic clue types developed, as outlined in earlier chapters. With the two exceptions of the cryptic definition, and the & Lit. clue, every cryptic clue type has, as a minimum, two elements, namely a definition of the answer and an alternative way of generating the answer. Without exception, the clue must contain a fair definition, so I'll begin by outlining what that fairness entails.

ADEQUATE DEFINITION

There are several general forms of definition, which I can illustrate by the word HORSE, definable directly as "steed" (synonym), "animal" (inclusion in superordinate category), "bay, perhaps" (definition by example, with an indication thereof), or indirectly, for example "price once offered for kingdom" (based on a familiar quotation).

The definition should be accurate. This statement appears obvious, but there are flawed definitions for answers or parts of answers that turn up in many crosswords. I do not accept that "keep" is an adequate synonym for "castle", however often it is implied in clues. Another example that comes to mind is defining RATEL as a sort of badger. The fact that another word for that creature is "honey-badger" and it is described as "badger-like" does not make it a badger any more than a guinea pig is a pig. Likewise, a lamprey may be eel-like, but that does not make it an eel.

More frequent are flawed definitions of shorter words that often form parts of answers: an IOU is not a bill, and an ion is not a charge.

At one point, I experienced a rash of dubious definitions for "tor", such as "eminence". "Eminence" is defined as "a piece of rising ground" and "tor" as "a hill or rocky peak", not a good enough match, in my opinion.

Another situation that arises is when the everyday and technical meanings of words differ. A master brewer informed us that "porter" is not "ale". He explained that ale is either pale or brown beer, whereas porter and stout are black beers. On the other hand, *Collins English Dictionary* defines "porter" as "a dark sweet ale brewed from black malt". A professor of English Literature wrote succinctly to me as follows: "Dear Sir, A codex is not a volume", pointing out that a codex is in book form (ie, pages placed on top of each other) whereas a volume consists, in accordance with its etymology, of rolled paper or other material. However, *Collins English Dictionary* and *Chambers* both define "codex" as a sort of volume, implying that the technical distinction has become blurred.

Extra care may be needed in defining words that fall into special categories, such as archaisms, poetic words, words or usages that are Scottish, American, and so on. If possible, an indication as to the special nature of the word is an appropriate fairness to the solver. Thus GANG (as a Scottish word) could be defined by "go North of the border", MEET (as an archaic adjective) as "no longer considered suitable" and DERBY (as an American name for a hat) as "at meeting, American might tip this".

Finally, a definition must be grammatically correct. In particular, it must be possible to interpret the definition as the appropriate part of speech. A specific grammatical error in crosswords that often occurs in crosswords that are not carefully edited is exemplified by:

Wine can be easy to transport (8)

Here the intended breakdown includes "can be" = "able". However, this supposed equivalence fails the "substitution test": try finding a sentence in which "can be" can be replaced by "able" and still make sense.

DOUBLE AND MULTIPLE DEFINITIONS

Polysemy in a word enables the most direct form of cryptic elaboration of a straight definitional clue, namely to put together two definitions. Thus, the words GANG, MEET, and DERBY all have alternative definitions to those just given, and using contrasting definitions we can construct a clue in each case, respectively:

A lot of criminals go North of the border (4)
Gathering for hunt no longer considered suitable (4)
At meeting, American might tip this for the big race (5)

Double definition clues qualify as cryptic since (by definition!) each such clue contains a definition and an alternative indication of the answer – which happens, in this case, to be another definition. The dedicated setter constructing such a clue will search for pairs of definitions that meet standards of accuracy but also combine one or more of the following features:

(a) contrast – the two definitions should not be too similar

(b) compatibility – fitting together in a sentence or phrase that makes good sense

(c) crypticity, in terms of each separate definition and/or the combination suggesting a misleading context

The expert setter always keeps in mind the question "How different do the definitions need to be?" In the extreme case, a clue such as:

Observe state (7)

combines two definitions that are too close, with the result that the solver could not be sure whether the answer should be COMMENT, DECLARE, MENTION or even possibly WITNESS. At the other extreme, it would be possible to take the position of a purist and only allow two definitions that have distinct etymological roots. However, this criterion I consider too severe. It would unnecessarily rule out many clues such as:

   Polish fan (4)

since, as analysed earlier (see p. 22), both meanings of "buff" derive from the same root.

Double definition clues provide many of the most succinct clues, since the basic requirement may be met by two or three words, or even a single hyphenated word:

   City-state (10)
   High-spirited (4)
   House-masters (5)
   Idle head (4)
   Medicine man (7)
   Behind one's back (6)
   Hue and cry (6)

In other cases, the definitions may be more elaborate and cryptic:

   Pools entries making one a rich man (5)
   Saw projections giving effective power (5)
   Drove dangerously and asked to be excused (3,2)
   On a trip, far away from base (4)
   Drivers try to avoid this carriage (4)

Often, particularly with phrases, a combination of literal and whimsical definitions is apposite:

   Information on position for patient? (3,11)
   Conversely, where one reckons to be after five? (2,3,5,4)
   How chess players regard each other, in general (6,3,5)
   Comfortable job for a boring person? (4-2-2)

An obvious extension, possible with some words, is to provide not two, but three – or even more – definitions. Bearing in mind the three distinct etymologies of "race" (see p. 21), that word could be clued as:

Run some ginger group of similar people (4)

Here is a clue (admittedly contrived) with no less than six distinct definitions:

Plant sailing vessel on the left to prick salmon in top condition (4)

THE CRYPTIC DEFINITION

As mentioned in Chapter 2, ambiguity at the sentence level is exploited in a type of clue that I regard as quintessential of *The Times* crossword from its earliest years, a tradition I strove to maintain. In many cases, a witticism of this nature can be directly transformed into a crossword clue. For example, the classic punning definition of "keelhaul" may be echoed in a clue thus:

Punitively put man under a hardship, so to speak (8)

The wonderful *Devil's Dictionary* by Ambrose Bierce contains many humorous definitions that border on the cryptic and could almost serve verbatim as crossword clues, thus:

*A costume sometimes worn by Scotchmen in America and
  Americans in Scotland (4)
A person who talks when you wish him to listen (4)
The kind of ignorance distinguishing the studious (8)
Mistaken at the top of one's voice (8)*

Particularly subtle examples of cryptic definitions, some vintage, some more recent, include:

Die of cold (3-4)
Weapon that quickens the pulse (3-7)
Lay down life for another (5-5)
The result of another's incapacity, as a rule (7)
A widespread belief (10)
New Jersey, for example (4)
Non-alcoholic drink sold in bars (9)
Manage to see what someone is saying? (7)
What could make party go with a swing? (9)
No reply comes to this player's address (9)
One may have to be satisfied with a second helping (8)
Heaviest casualties of D-Day? (4-6)
It probably entails an evening out (3,2,8)
Mug presented at christening? (4-4)

& LIT CLUES

This class of clues constitutes the second exception to the general rule that a cryptic clue contains a juxtaposition of a definition and a second indication of the answer. In this case, the general rule is broken in the sense that the two parts of the clue are not side-by-side but coincident. Consider the following:

What might get me in post improperly (8)

Here the anagram indicator "improperly", in conjunction with a group of words with the necessary number of letters for the answer, stands out prominently. A rearrangement of "me in post" yields NEPOTISM. "What might get" are acceptable "filler words" that refer to the process leading from the anagram to the solution. Now consider the whole sentence literally. It provides, I hope you agree, a fair definition of "nepotism" (the etymology of which word is, en passant, interesting). Thus, an "& lit" clue is one which indicates, by way of an anagram or other device, how to construct a word or phrase, and – when re-read *in toto* – literally defines that word or phrase.

This type of clue is highly regarded by setters, and there is certainly a lot of satisfaction in manipulating the elements of a clue so that they work well for both the build-up and the definition. Here are some of my favourite examples (you will see that they are most frequently based on anagrams):

A form of DG, Yanks having it? (12,3)
(DG is an abbreviation for *Deo gratias*, meaning "thanks be to God")
Hood's resort few disturbed (8,6)
Take sweetheart and run (5)
Odd if no males could be found here! (4,2,3)
Pole 'n' wire arranged to provide this? (5,4)
It can give actors no end of excitement (5)
For whom right and wrong can go in ledger (9,5)
Each MP needs one composed (6,6)
River? Hardly! (4)
Set many free (7)

And here is a rara avis that could be classified as "lit & lit":

One shot with craft on course (9)

Chapter 5

ARS MAGNA

As sketched in Chapter 2, the history of the great art (*ars magna*) of anagrams is as fascinating as it is long.

It's highly likely that you know that "Honor est a Nilo" is an anagram for Horatio Nelson, and "We all make his praise" for William Shakespeare, but can you identify other notables from the following anagrams?

Greatest born idealist
Govern, clever lad
Radium came
Person whom all read
Laud'd Norseman

Traditionally, the most highly regarded anagrams were those that related to the word or phrase being rearranged. Here are some of the best:

Oft ruins me
Cost me time
Voices rant on
I'm dot in place
Tender name

BASIC STRUCTURE OF ANAGRAM CLUES

The invention of the crossword provided a natural habitat for anagrams. They initially appeared blatantly flagged by "(anag.)" and unencumbered by a definition of the answer, but evolved into the more interesting form we know today. A standard anagram clue, by contemporary standards, consists of a definition of the answer (coming at the beginning or end of the clue), the letters to be rearranged (generally as one or more consecutive words), and an anagram indicator, ie, some word or phrase that suggests rearrangement.

The variety of words and phrases that may be pressed into service as anagram indicators is enormous, and the following list is certainly only a haphazard sample:

perhaps, possibly, potentially, somehow, otherwise, in a way
sort of, form of, version of
could become, might be, could make
odd, strange, abnormal, funny, silly, novel, revolutionary
mad, crazy, wild, excited
wrong, misdirected, out of order
wrongly, mistakenly, strangely, originally
calamitously, disastrously
confused, rearranged, at sea, agitated, convoluted, in disarray
damaged, ruined, broken, ill-treated
drunk, tipsy, befuddled
altered, rewritten, composed, ordered, arranged, broadcast
bad, awful, badly, terribly

Whereas, as exemplified by the above list, most anagram indicators are adjectives, adverbs, or past tenses of verbs, I see no reason to rule out the appropriate use of nouns for this purpose, as in this example:

A pectoral disaster for her (9)

As an editor, I was very critical of what I called "sore-thumb" anagrams, ie, clues where the anagram stood out like that distressed digit. Conversely, from the setter's perspective, there's an art in selecting an anagram indicator that fits seamlessly with the anagram constituents and definition:

Granted me burial at sea, where may sailors have died? (7,8)
Refuse collector shifted deal of old litter (6,9)
Sing a carol arranged for this instrument (3,7)
Champion in a sport got knocked out (11)
He's needed to get the classroom in order (12)

VARIATIONS AND ELABORATIONS

Sometimes it's necessary to carry out some pre-processing of the ingredients before mixing them, for example by gathering words together:

Compose duet with me for singing in church (2,4)
Adjust, as a rule, and get organised (8)
Sink with a tap rigged up in the country (8)

or by shortening or abbreviating one or more of the words:

Aunt Sally quickly cooked fruit (7)
Company director – one involved with Paris and Rome (10)
Singular crowd puller? Not half! (5,3)

or otherwise (the last is especially tricky):

Explorer in triple North Sea disaster (6)
Composure as majority of Labour MP changed (6)
Cat he twice confused – a wild one (7)
Author upset W. B., for example, twice or three times (6,6)

In other cases, one anagram may be included in, or juxtaposed with, another:

Singer that's old-fashioned in changing times (8)
German people go to resort in outlandish shorts (10)
Main change with altered set of policy proposals (9)

The following is a very special case, exploiting an unusual feature of a word:

Given two orders, a rep means to come back (8)

On rare occasions, a word lends itself to a form of anagram in which the ingredients are doubled:

All-round competition he can't hold candle to, doubly
    indisposed (9)
We hate what repeatedly ruins this crop (5)
Flag of gaol? Either half could do for prison (5)
Rebuild ruin – turn it into twice the city (5)
Is an occasion arrangeable to repeat this card game? (6)

Another subtle twist is to provide the solver with alternative anagrams:

European repeatedly adapted for Oriental relation (8)
Perversely start nine or ten trains passing (9)
Permit Oslo or Rome to slip badly as city (10)
Girl as model, or some lad, possibly (7)
Cab stolen or lost can be sorted out by one (9)

Finally, here is a collection of clues I term "inverse anagrams", for a reason that should become obvious:

Pet goat hungry hunter shouldn't have taken? (1,4,2,7)
One way to produce neat substitute? (9)
Striking successes – one way to get this? (5,4)
Fall asleep like Don, perhaps (3,3)
Wonderful score bringing me gain in game? (6,10)

FIRST TEST

All clues are of types described in Chapters 4 and 5.

ACROSS

1 Cook some meat in pan (5)
4 Relief from pain from a leg, as in a fracture (9)
9 Composing music for children (9)
10 Fish that's seen between two rays (5)
11 Information for betters racing tipster organised (8,5)
14 Remove from position disturbing to us (4)
15 Arrangement of tapestries that's barely finished (10)
18 From rigs, traced order for explosive cases (10)
19 Queen needed for trick (4)
21 Where people train for submarine trip to Europe (7,6)
24 Bail I arranged as possibility for defence (5)
25 Plant in arid region desperate to propagate? (6,3)
27 Sort of drive chiefly relied on (5-4)
28 The more someone has of them, the more he wants (5)

DOWN

1 Leading vehicle close lorry might crash into (5,5)
2 Sharp implement used by worker at last, breaking law (3)
3 Areas in which pamphlets may be found (6)
4 Created hostility as a dateline is changed (9)
5 Slave whose relations were fabulous (5)
6 How the second half of a crossword is formed? (8)
7 Divisive policy Saint George reformed (11)
8 Cuts lines at right angles in graph (4)
12 Taking a theoretical view of theft? (10)
13 The port of Salerno, possibly? (3,7)
16 Dailies rubbished by editor as too good to be true (9)
17 As to *Air on G string*, a change for this musician repeated (8)
20 Perform miles better than someone else, for example (6)
22 New name for Diana? (5)
23 Light entertainment of moderate quality (4)
26 Another bird found where dozens of blackbirds were (3)

Chapter 6

THE ART OF CAMOUFLAGE

Which Scandinavian city is in a central European country? The answer is provided by one of the best known of all crossword clues:

City in Czechoslovakia (4)

If I were to meet a keen solver, I might report the encounter thus:

Composer of some crosswords met an aficionado (7)

The above are examples of clues in which the answer is embedded within one or more words of the clue.

BASIC STRUCTURE OF HIDDEN CLUES

A standard hidden clue has the usual two-part structure, definition and secondary indication. The latter is made up of a word or group of words in which the answer is embedded, together with an indication of the embedding. In *Times* style (which not all crosswords follow) strictly no superfluous words are allowed (a principle that applies to clues in general). To cite an extreme example:

Priest caught up in charge of the Light Brigade (3)

has three words which cannot be structurally justified.

By convention, punctuation in the embedding set of words may be ignored as long as the letters of the answer appear in order. If the answer is a proper noun, and so begins with a capital letter, it is considered allowable that this letter in the clue is in lower case (as in both examples quoted at the start). Further, the answer must be genuinely embedded, ie, not start at the beginning of a word or end at the end of a word.

Hidden clues, by their nature, are liable to be relatively easy, since the word is staring the solver in the face, and it is relatively difficult for the setter to disguise the form of the clue. For this reason, it has been conventional to limit their use in *Times* puzzles to at most one per puzzle. In the following, the presence of giveaway words such as "some", "part of" conveys a clear signal:

Some clips of actors shown thereby (4,5)
Part of cash I posted in packet, perhaps (4)
Some guns heathen wanted to bring out for fighting (9)
Opera producer wants clever diva in part (5)

Even with minimal indicators such as "in", the structure tends to be obvious:

Immediate reply in letter I posted (7)
Musical piece from player on double-bass (5)
Lamb, for example, in casseroles, say, is tasty (8)
Source of critical comments – from Fabian, not a Tory (9)

Nevertheless, a degree of camouflage is possible by subtly varying the phrasing:

Given a choice, pick out a bit of Mexican food (5)
Oriental work which ingeniously reveals the answer (1,5)
Hungry hunter tucked into the sausages (4)
Give no medicine containing such poisonous stuff (5)

Aesthetically, it is satisfying to find a hidden answer spanning several words in the clue, while not leaping out at the solver. The best examples I know are:

Some job at hand? We'll soon see (4,3,5)

which combines a five-word embedding phrase with a one-word definition, while still making acceptable sense, and:

Sensation concealed by Chopin, Sand – needlessly (4,3,7)

Also pleasing is when a hidden clue is an "& lit" clue (see p. 68):

It is used in Tripoli by a native (6)
Occupant of larger nest (4)
Part of sacred orthodoxy (5)

VARIATIONS

The most common variant is when the word is embedded backwards, the indication of which may depend on whether it is an across clue or a down clue. Attention to detail is important in this case. For example, it would be illogical to propose the following:

VIP held up by delay, originally (5) [D]

since "delay, originally" is horizontal, so does not hold ROYAL up. However, it is not difficult to remove this flaw, for example, by changing the clue to:

VIP held back by delay, originally (5)

for <u>either</u> an across or a down clue. On the other hand:

Some delay originally upset VIP (5) [D]

is fine, since the instruction is to remove ROYAL from the horizontal "delay originally" and then place it, upset, in the grid.

Various phrases can fairly indicate an answer hidden backwards or upwards as the case may be:

Some Socialists turned back outside the Ministry (4) [A]
Fired again, in retreat from hostile rebels (5) [A]
Some panic if I capsize, swept back into the ocean (7) [A]
Piece of music put back in programme – open otherwise (4-4)
Some horrific scenes turned up in futuristic work (3-2) [D]
They're found in returning, perhaps, to origins (5)

Other variations are rarer, but occasionally a word lends itself to being hidden twice:

Fabric repeatedly found in sale, not economical enough (4)
Warnings repeatedly coming from women, so men stop (5)
She's repeatedly kept in bed – it helped, I think (5)
Record error derisively – double entry system's what you need (5)

and here is another twist:

Row back and forth in boat if fitter (4)

and one more:

Carry too far out of Dover – twice (6)

Further help can be given the solver by indicating not only the hidden answer, but also its packaging:

For winter coming, install this telephone system in part of
*   house (8)*
Play included by author to make Peking learn (4,4)
Could be the lad put her in bad position? (5)

A final example of a refinement shows how a specific property of the embedding may be exploited to help the clue read coherently:

As centre half in match, I seldom cheat (6)

Chapter 7

CONSTRUCTION KITS

In this chapter, I deal with several ways of assembling answers by manipulating components. As described in Chapter 2, such clues have precursors in charades and rebuses, and in puzzles involving reversals and palindromes.

ADDITION

Clues in which words are split into two and each part as well as the whole is defined are direct descendants of charades. The definitions of the parts may simply be juxtaposed, or there may be appropriate filler words describing the juxtaposition or, in the case of down clues, the placing of one part above or below the other. Here are some examples:

Flier in jet going over the top (8) [D]
Part of the orchestra showed emotion, affected by moving air (9)
Dame selecting actors for a variety of entertainment (12)
Notable courtship combined hearts, perhaps (5,4)
Find musical entertainment jolly (9)
Chap promises to pay back without interest (7)

A straightforward extension is to split the word into more than two parts:

Pictures, poem, and book as human creations (9)
One part of bridge is twitching, resisting all control (11)
Rested at home with disease that's making one unconscious (6,3)
Eccentric provided land and inspiration for sports ground (7,4,4)

Sometimes the parts form a coherent phrase:

> *One who's willing to try a peak (8)*
> *Christian's statement of his position in Muslim country (7)*
> *Violent commotion has potential to attract attention (6)*
> *Find similar wood for a small container (8)*
> *Beggar's confession of being incorrigible? (9)*

Occasionally a word in the clue may be divided, turned into synonyms, and reassembled:

> *Criminal from Leatherhead (9)*
> *Alternative suggestion from bartender (7-8)*

Another twist is when the answer consists of two or more words which need to be regrouped:

> *Bill's initial appearance, walking under trees (5,7) [D]*
> *Try going in a certain direction that's very sad (5-7)*
> *Has impressive gear to chop down tree (4,1,4)*

INSERTION

Words may be combined, alternatively, by inserting one inside the other – or, looking at it the other way, putting one around the other. For fairness, of course, there must be an indication of this insertion or circumscription, which may be as simple as "in" or "around", respectively, or more subtle. Here is a selection:

> *Old actor finding something amusing in dance (7,8)*
> *Month in which libertine enters African city (9)*
> *Story about jet flier in conflict (10)*
> *It may contain brief accounts of old man in famous case (7)*

(Note, in the last clue above, the filler word "case" which allows the clue to make sense and is justified as an indication of the word that takes the role of container.)

As a variant, the insertion may be piecewise, if this is fairly indicated:

> *Fools inserting it repeatedly between points (7)*
> *Italian city in parts stuck into sea (5)*

In some cases, the sense may be improved by specifying the nature of the insertion more precisely:

> *Station us below head in school (6) [D]*

SUBTRACTION

Like numbers, words may be subtracted as well as added. In this type of clue, the solver is provided with two words – either directly or through a definition – one of which forms part of the other and a definition of the answer that results by removing that part, as in these examples:

> *Thinks about abolishing rate for French composer (7)*
> *Sign office staff don't keep secret (5)*
> *Singer in state of nudity? Get her off! (4)*
> *Footwear that's wrecked, not aged (5)*
> *Frenchman disrobes his revolutionary leader (6)*

REVERSAL

Words that can be reversed to form other words are a boon to the setter. The components of a clue exploiting this property are a definition of the answer, a definition of its reversed form, and an indication that a reversal is necessary. The indication of reversal needs to take account of whether the clue is down or across. Across clues can be back, going West, in retreat, and so on. Down clues can be up, heading North, be raised, and so on. Other indications, such as "reversed" will work for either down or across. Here are some examples:

> *Save from boat capsizing (3) [D]*
> *Going the wrong way, falls again to spinner (6)*
> *Showing a little bit of character, is inspiring in retreat (5) [A]*
> *Did some work at last, having turned up in Greek island (5) [D]*

The setter may need to be careful not to break the principle that a clue should not have more than one valid answer, which can happen if the indication of reversal is placed in the middle. For example, in this clue:

> *Cad, returning, joins up again (7) [A]*

it is not clear whether the first word defined or the second is to be reversed. The flaw is easily remedied by amending the clue to one of the following:

> *Returning cad joins up again (7) [A]*
> *Cad joins up again, having returned (7) [A]*

The raw material to be reversed does not have to be a single word:

> *Court action making offence clear? Just the reverse (6)*
> *Exotic drama we are mounting? Butler did it! (7) [D]*
> *Not a stone – contrariwise, an enormous weight (7)*
> *Was no safety device set up for this cutting tool? (5,3) [D]*
> *Communist Party's comeback is more surprising (5) [A]*
> *Theatrical character a couple expected to follow up (5) [D]*

Palindromes represent another class of words with a very special property that calls out to be recognised and exploited. For fairness, of course, the palindromic structure must be indicated, and the setter seeks ways to achieve this which combine fairness with lack of sore-thumb obviousness:

Not an irreversible mistake (4)
Like Janus, looking both ways (7)
Unaffected by reversal, as a principle (5)
Language unaffected by backwardness in spelling (9)

Chapter 8
SOUND CLUES

The English language is rich in homophones, words that are pronounced the same but spelt differently. As an Irishman, I had to adjust to the fact that, for the English, a pair of words like "for" and "four", which to my ear are as distinct as "far" and "fare", sound the same. To this day, I find it strange to pronounce "cheater" like "cheetah".

Basic Structure of Homophone Clues

Cryptic clues that exploit words sounding the same may be construed as sound-based puns adapted to the two-part structure of definition and secondary indication. The secondary indication, in this case, consists of a definition of a homophone of the answer and an indicator of homophony. The use of stock phrases such as "we hear" means that clues based on this device are often easy to spot:

> *Bad feeling produced by arrest, it's said (6)*
> *Audibly one affected by illness in chest (6)*
> *Sound head needed for political group (4)*
> *Planet revolved rapidly, we hear (5)*
> *We may hear a lot from this social gathering (4)*

Consequently, setters try to find indicators that, while fair, are not glaringly obvious:

> *Report from another country? Japan, possibly (6)*
> *Singer's second lowest note in audition (5)*
> *Skill that's not at all pronounced (4-3)*

A technical point observed by the careful setter is, in accordance with the general principle that a clue should lead to only one reasonable answer, to avoid ambiguity that can result if the homophone indicator is placed as the central component in the clue. Consider:

Check, we hear, possible weather forecast (4)

Here the solver does not know whether the "we hear" should be associated with the first definition or the second, and consequently has no basis for deciding between two equally valid answers (and this ambiguity will not be resolved if the second letter is unchecked). It is a simple matter to remove the ambiguity by modifying the clue to one of the following:

Reportedly check possible weather forecast (4)
Check possible weather forecast, we hear (4)

VARIATIONS

In some clues, the word is split into two parts, one of which is indicated by a definition and the other by a definition of a homophone, as in these examples:

Cat reportedly on watch for bird (9) (D)
Flood covering Florence, say (8)

In others, each of the two parts is homophonically indicated:

Anti-intellectual female relative of Gertrude, say (10)
Young girl bound, we hear, to be suspicious (8)
Essayist and poet, say, put in the shade (5-4)
Sampling of opinion produced by high-speed staff, say (6,4)

The sounds of letters, as opposed to words, may also be exploited, usually to indicate a part of the answer:

Tropical country you said is in new Caribbean plan (6,8)

Occasionally, a word lends itself to being completely clued in this fashion (see p. 29 for another example):

Say, are you M? Then be followed by a number of Cubans (5)
Are you the person elected, so to speak, for this seat? (4)
His spelling's sound in essays I see about (5)
Oh! I see you are pronounced out of order – that's rare (5)

Another type of clue (not universally admired) based on homophones requires homophonic pre-processing of words in the clue, as in:

Reported naval exercise in the Middle East (5,5)
Artistic old lady making a profit, so to speak (5)
Poet's rhyme we hear (5)
I'll cite insane pronouncement locating this famous building (5,4)

the latter being the clue that, to my mind, most resembles a traditional pun.

The following combines two uses:

One who acquires a farm building (as opposed to cellar), say (5)

The opposite of a homophone is a heteronym, that is, one of two or more words spelt the same way but pronounced differently. A word with this property also affords the opportunity for a cryptic clue:

Artist's a saint? Doesn't sound like it (5)
Executes females? Not from what we hear (4)
Disputed what crew did? Doesn't sound like it (5)

A final example that is unique in its conception is the following:

Poetic device exemplified in Keats and Yeats (3-5)

SECOND TEST

All clues in this puzzle are of types described in Chapters 6-8.

ACROSS

1 Liberal following warning about vote, say (3,7)

7 Burden carried by wagon, usually (4)

9 Try to find from where we hear repeated notes (8)

10 About to form an association – is that so? (6)

11 Operatic singer insensitive to listeners (6)

12 In speech, provokes glimpses of understanding (8)

13 Watch just part of movie – Western (4)

15 Run away with one friend without breaking the law (10)

18 Single-minded about time, like day and night (10)

20 Gas turbine only partly used (4)

21 Feeling tension, with final courses going the wrong way (8)

24 Coin contained by a small opening (6)

26 Maintaining exactly the same course in sound or channel (6)

27 Bill and I draw off contaminated water (4,4)

28 At one time, part of initiation ceremony (4)

29 Announced in diplomatic style, bit by bit (10)

DOWN

2 Choice about time for medical treatment (9)

3 Peer at home among the quality (5)

4 Taunts all, yet only some become target for criticism (4,5)

5 Taking short-term view and maximising performance, say (7)

6 Makes vessels for the tea trade, so to speak (5)

7 Primate needs to call up religious type in Ireland (9)

8 A place for sleeping in France, in the dark (5)

14 Reportedly pierce part of canvas, on a large scale (9)

16 Removed from contest if I err as witness (9)

17 After short time, spot one bird or another (9)

19 Trials resulting from trade with gold (7)

22 Person with enormous power to increase tension in hearing (5)

23 Put in position to be either noticed or mentioned, we hear (5)

25 Measure for Russians clever Stalinists have introduced (5)

Chapter 9
SHREDS AND PATCHES

The preceding chapters have painted an idealised picture, in that the examples provided fit cleanly into a range of distinctive clue types. However, typically when one is facing the task of cluing the words in a completed crossword grid, a sizeable proportion are not so tractable as to fit any obvious template. In these circumstances, the setter improvises by patching together bits and pieces and/or combining cluing devices in more complex constructions.

BITS AND PIECES

The resourceful setter has many ways to cope with a single extraneous letter. In particular, abbreviations prove very convenient when the addition or insertion of a single letter is required, as in:

Great excitement about black flower (9)
Perform badly and lose, with little change after first half (7)
Welsh agreeing to meet in English town (6)

Alternatively, the single letter may be subtracted. The removal of a specified letter is reminiscent of the device employed in rebuses of showing a letter crossed out, as in these examples:

Selfishness can make one run away from disease (7)
Played foolishly, discarding king? That's rich! (7)
Yokels left out of joke (9)

A check of the *Collins English Dictionary*, *Concise Oxford Dictionary*, and *Chambers Dictionary* reveals a surprising degree of inconsistency in the abbreviations that they list. Take the letter B, for example. At least in the editions I have to hand, Chambers lists several words that B is an abbreviation for that are not listed by the other two, including Baron, Britain, and barrel(s). *Collins* is particularly comprehensive and, alone of the three has, for example, bay, Bible, balboa, belga, and bolivar. Even the abbreviationally abstemious COD manages to allow barn(s) (unit of area in particle physics), absent from the others. Indeed, the dictionaries are not always even internally consistent – *Chambers* has C, D, and H for clubs, hearts, and diamonds, but not S for spades. Accordingly, *The Times* Crossword is relatively conservative, only allowing abbreviations (of one or more letters) that are common to all three dictionaries or, in the judgment of the editor, are sufficiently well known (such as C, D, H, S for the card suits, even though only *Chambers* (almost) lists them). For example, the approved list for B is: blood group, note or key, bishop, British, black, boron, billion, book, born, bowled, breadth, bye, bachelor.

As well as abbreviations, there are a number of ways of indicating individual letters by symbols. These include the familiar Roman numerals (I, V, X, L, C, D, M), c = speed of light (sometimes clued as "maximum possible speed") and K for 1000 (accepted as a result of common usage, though originally 1024 = 2 to the power 10). O can be indicated by "zero", "duck", "love" and so on, or anything reflecting its circular shape (such as "ring", "circle", even "circular letter"). X can be a vote or a kiss, "times" (as in multiplication), or one of the invaluable trio of unknowns, x, y, and z.

A combination of lexicographical consensus and the editor's judgment governs also which longer abbreviations are acceptable. The following clues provide examples:

Monarch's contributed to tax, in practice (8)
Refusal, for example, to follow leader in race (8)
Best policy is to lose stone, darling (5)
Publicity dreadful female needed to get on (8)

Old weapon found in church somewhere in Derbyshire (9)
Saw dog restrained by lead (7)

The ramifications of abbreviations are too many and complex to allow a comprehensive analysis, so I will deal only with a few salient examples.

For some reason, the ubiquitous defining of the letter L in crosswords as "novice", "beginner", "neophyte", "student" and so on has always irritated me. L is specifically a learner driver. "Learner" is an adequate definition, but the others just listed I regard as stretched to an unacceptable degree. Accordingly, when I was in a position to make arbitrary judgments, I usually took a hard line on this particular point.

N, S, E, and W are flexible friends of the setter, since they can be defined in several ways – as points, directions, quarters, poles (for N and S). Their significance in relation to bridge can also be used, though I expect something more precise than the mere "player" to indicate one of them. I also recognise that a case can be made for "hand" as a definition in the context of bridge, but did not allow it.

It is extremely stingy to offer the solver "state" and expect her or him to work out which of the many possibilities is indicated. Even considering only the United States (and there are other countries with states, of course) this leaves her or him with a choice of well over fifty possibilities (since many states have alternative abbreviations). If possible, in my view, the setter should narrow down the number of possibilities by refining the definition to, say "Western state" (which has a degree of crypticity to it, into the bargain).

As well as abbreviations and symbols, there are many other ways of indicating single letters. Beginnings and ends of words are the most common. The first letter of a word can be indicated by words such as "beginning of", "originally", "head", and so on. (The convention found in some other crosswords that "bit of", or similar expressions, points to the first letter of a word has always struck me as illogical. I see no strong reason why "bit of cheese" is C rather than H, E or S – or indeed HE). Similarly, the last letter can be signalled by "end", "conclusion" and so on. More generally, the middle letter, second letter, and so on may be indicated as in the following examples where the single letter forms part of a build-up by addition, insertion or subtraction:

Reveals, around radioactive core, such emissions? (4,4)
Most original of Carroll's characters – mad type and rabbit (7)
Darling child has to travel to journey's end (5)
Had a row with second in command, a leftist (5)
Part of army has no end of fighting in Europe (9)
Comprehensive school's head showing distress (8)

As a cultural group, Cockneys, because of their distinctive speech patterns, feature disproportionately in crosswords, mostly in clues requiring the omission of one particular letter:

As Eliza appeared to Higgins, and vice versa, we hear (7)
Poor German's at his work place, according to Cockney (14)
Difficult time for Doolittle to show passion (6)
King resembling chess set in Looking-glass 'ouse? (6)
Bow and arrow found in my city, one might say (7)

In other cases, only the location of a letter to be removed is indicated:

Italian duke cut flower (7)
Discovering front's missing, narrowly averted disaster (4,5) [A]
Eastern commander using firearm heartlessly (6)

As a special case, words with doubled letters in the middle may be exploited in the following manner:

Half-heartedly interfere with count, for example (5)

A range of manoeuvres is possible to cope with pairs of letters or longer word-fragments. For example, a pair of letters may be indicated as the ends of a word, or two or more letters could be indicated by the middle of a word:

Happy with what's contained by England's borders (9)
Trifles with violent murderer in extremes of ferocity (8)
Widely applicable information provided by Central American (7)
With two of hearts, battle to produce trick after this (3,6)

In other cases, taking half of a word may be useful:

German government half affected by the spirit of yesterday? (4,4)
Argue with daughter in pursuit of pleasure? Not half! (5)
Left-winger runs to kick left half (7)

A word shortened by one letter at the beginning, middle or end may be a convenient part of a build-up. The word to be depleted may be provided directly, or indirectly through definition:

Taking only a little time to get excited, mostly (7)
Model made by author of horse, not quite finished (9)
Sorry about pie, not altogether nice to eat (5)
Fare for Japanese coming from America in vessel that's docked (5)
Wretched chap losing head? Not so! (7)
Box in half-hearted manner in city (10)

PICKING AND CHOOSING

In more recent times, setters have developed a range of clues that depend entirely on the selection of letters from words in the clue, in one way or another. A particularly useful device for words that are otherwise intractible is the acronym, in which the first letters of a succession of words are taken. The clue, of course, must plainly indicate that this is being done, which is not easy to disguise. Accordingly, there should be no more than one such clue in any crossword. Variants are when final letters are taken, or, less commonly, central letters, or some combination. Here is a mixed selection of clues using these constructions:

*Assembling contents of the job lot, the man makes such
    a fuss (3-2)*
Weapon featured in Casebook of Sherlock Holmes, *initially (4)*
A source of notes of Bank of England, initially (4)
Individual doing little except rest, primarily (5)
Conclusions reached by board move team to protest (4)
Long journey starts in the rain and ends in the dark (4)

Other clues take letters from the ends of one or more words, again with an appropriate indication that this is to be done:

Extreme characters in England greatly affected by anxiety (4)
Dorothy's skirts are so smart (5)
River Trent's edges (4)
Unloading left, right and centre in this country (6)

Another device is to juxtapose a number of words with their first letters, or last letters, removed:

Nine or ten one had beheaded (6)
Starts off paper by foolishly copying others (5)
Language that is clipped (4)
Up at farm, big man heads off these birds (9)

Yet another form of selection is exemplified in these clues:

Composer and arranger being oddly selective (4)
Child that's unruly and aberrant – nothing odd in that (4)
Select even parts of strongest gear (4)
Stuff to rub bows, and even parts of arrows, in (5)
Odd bits of culture, such as this (4)

And here are some more unusual examples of being selective:

Damage by fire headquarters of Scottish orthodox churches (6)
Vessel that's two parts out of the water (4)

COMPLEX CONSTRUCTIONS

The various construction methods set out in Chapter 7 may be
exploited in combination. Consider this clue:

Skilfully holding back confusion in meeting (8)

The build-up for ASSEMBLY requires both a reversal (of MESS)
and an inclusion (in ABLY).

Here are some other examples involving combinations of
construction methods:

Carriage taking hard-hearted father to school (7)
Race run by university the wrong way (5)
Places where Mexican food's gobbled up by animals (9) [D]
Poisonous stuff put into blend, in particular (8)
Flower bringing back pain after Pa suffers a loss (8)
There's no sin in doctor using this (4)

HYBRIDS

Expecially when faced with words that do not readily lend themselves
to straightforward cluing by a standard method, the setter often resorts
to hybridisation. Hybrid clues consist of two or more components,
each of which may be indicated through definition, anagram, reversal,
homophone (if a word) or through abbreviation or symbol, selection,
etc. (if a word-fragment) and which are assembled through addition,
insertion, subtraction or a mixture thereof, as in:

It takes more than vodka to get Red Army drunk (6,4)

Island fellow diary recollected (3,6)
Display what's provided in, say, main street (8)
Contest round both ends of the pool involved in this (5-4)
Bishop travels amid confusion – who looks after the train? (10)
One who advises consumers to decline an artistic shade of red, say (9)

MULTI-STEP CLUES

The prudent setter, when composing a grid, tries to avoid words that are going to prove intractable. This aim is not always achieved, of course, and one may finish up with a word like HIBISCUS. Here is one possibility:

Plant making hot biscuits poorly, short of time

It has the merit, at least, that it paints a reasonably plausible picture of a factory turning out fresh cookies under pressure, and not making too good a job of it. However, as a clue it has an inelegant complexity with the solver required to:

Interpret "hot" as its abbreviation H
Interpret "time" as its abbreviation T
Take T out of BISCUITS
Form an anagram of BISCUIS
Combine H and IBISCUS

Such multi-step clues should be kept to a minimum, and when they are unavoidable, they should be assembled to read as coherently and meaningfully as possible. Here are two further examples which, I think, work quite well despite their complexity:

Result of cutting off fashionable female's quarter inch in
*   length (14)*
Raised one card-player endlessly, with king and four aces (8) [D]

Chapter 10
IMPROVING YOUR GAME

As stated at the outset, there is no danger that explanation of the main types of clue will dull the challenge of crosswords. Rather it will, I hope, put you in a position to appreciate their subtleties more deeply while still meeting new challenges daily. If you began as a beginner and have thoroughly digested the foregoing chapters, you should be roughly in the position of a chess or bridge player who has mastered the basics. To progress to expert status, you will have to learn many more moves and ploys and play a lot more against strong opposition.

Like the language itself, and indeed any complex intellectual activity, crosswords continuously evolve. Words drop out of use or change their meanings; new words and meanings take their place. The same applies to the popular and high culture forming the setter's and the solver's shared background. There is, of course, a core of unchanging knowledge, historical and geographical, intellectual achievements in literature, art and music of enduring familiarity. The solver is entitled to expect, and the crossword setter and editor is expected to pursue, a balance between tradition and innovation.

Cluing style also evolves. Compared with early *Times* puzzles, today's setters are more concerned with the nuts and bolts of technically sound clues. However, being technically sound, while necessary, is not sufficient. The tradition of *The Times* Crossword was built on wit, and that remains the most important objective.

In the more than three score years and ten in the life of cryptic crosswords, they have developed their own argot and conventions. Knowledge of these is part of what it takes to become a skilled solver. However, there are words, usages, and cultural references that continue to exist in crosswords long after they have largely disappeared elsewhere (one contributory factor is the mental longevity of crossword setters). As editor, I pursued a policy of phasing out some of the more obvious anachronisms, if for no other reason than respect for the next generation of solvers in their twenties or younger. These young people are unlikely to be familiar with much of the slang and other elements of popular culture that I grew up with. There is no particular reason why they should remember the Teddy boys of the 1950s or the beehive hairstyle of the 1960s. Likewise, it is necessary to judge which achievements in literature, art, and music that may have been prominent thirty or forty years ago remain so, and which works created since then may reasonably be expected to be in the knowledge base of the solver.

A comparison of the number of suitable words with the number of cryptic crosswords created in more than seventy years makes it obvious that any word in general usage over that period has been clued many, many times. A correspondent to *The Times* in 1959 wrote as follows:

I have amused myself recently by visualizing 'Crossword Country'. It consists largely of tors covered with heather (ling) and the predominating fauna are ernes, hens, lions, asps, and she-cats. They feed, as appropriately, on grubs, sole, bass, ants, bees, and each other. There are, unfortunately, also humans, all dastards, renegades or rips, except for some dons, doctors, Royal Engineers and tars (Abs). Their names are Mac, Ian or Eli …

Accordingly, the setter is constantly looking for new words and for fresh ways to treat old words. Experienced hands tend to avoid certain words that lend themselves to one, or a limited number of, treatments. I avoid including a certain word in any crossword grid I construct because the following clue for it makes it difficult to look for any alternative to the obvious:

Instant tea or coffee (5)

Almost any five-letter word beginning with E demands a special effort to be innovative – and is it possible to come up with a fresh clue for OKAPI?

Another preoccupation of conscientious setters is avoiding cliches like the plague. No doubt the definition of a river as a "runner" was once a creative act, but it has become the epitome of hackneyed cluing and should be used only as a last resort. Solvers rely on spotting reliable cues as to the construction of a clue. Accordingly, it is good to look for clues that keep them on their toes by the inclusion of a word or phrase that does not imply the usual construction. Consider the following clue:

Quarters, note, to the French (6)

At first sight, this looks like a collection of crossword cliches and the solver may try to fit together some combination of N, E, S, W (quarters), A, B, … G or DO, RE, MI, etc, (note) and AU (to the French). In fact, none of these standard responses is appropriate in this case.

In the following examples words that typically have the role of anagram indicator take instead the role of anagram ingredients:

A trifle that could disturb pickets, say (5,4)
Deep blue, perhaps, I altered (8)
Novel form of breathing, maybe (9,5)

Here are some other examples where the usual cues are misleading:

College men ever-present on board (5)
Possessions as revealed after end of life, say (6)
Youth leader in school adding twice as much (9)
Live under a tree, perhaps (5) [D]
Without any qualifications, say? Lady takes no notice (7)

PUSHING THE ENVELOPE

In the opening chapters, various guidelines for playing fair and for providing clues that make a pleasing sound when the penny drops were presented. Like ice-skating, crossword clues may be judged by the criteria of technical merit and artistic impression. Within the constraints imposed by the former, there is enormous scope for the exercise of the latter. This scope is illustrated by a mere sample of clue types that exemplify how the standard types of clue analysed in preceding chapters by no means exhaust the resources of the setter, thereby ensuring that originality in crosswords is in no danger of drying up. This sample demonstrates how the repertoire of standard clues may be extended with originality and fairness, always bearing in mind Afrit's Injunction that "you need not mean what you say, but you must say what you mean".

SHIFTS

An anagram may require minimal change, in that only one or two letters need to be repositioned, and a clue may exploit this property:

Axed when moving West (4)
Desire to work second shift in T-shirt (6)
Antipathy as head of gallery is replaced (7)
Ram cart with back to front vehicle (7) [A]
Do a heart transplant for Tom (5)
Resigned after editor's move to change structure (8)

DOUBLES

When a word or phrase consists of the same letters repeated, it is natural to exploit that structure:

Formidable person in two-man crew? (6)
Bear repeated ridicule (4-4)
Excited bridge player doubled experts (3,5)

> *Gun dogs (3-3)*
> *Highly confidential – still gets duplicated (4-4)*

PAIRS

A number of words and phrases split obligingly into two components that have something in common:

> *Early birds (4-4)*
> *Plant in which carriages are assembled (7)*
> *Blues used in service (5,4)*
> *Sorts of cheese found in part of London (5,7)*
> *So-called lady appearing in Mothers' Union (5)*
> *Appropriate appearance of two gifts (14)*
> *Repeated British exclamation of surprise (6)*
> *Two sorts of seamen easily disposed of (12)*

YES AND NO

On occasions, a phrase may provide a definition of the answer, and at the same time, taken differently, as a secondary indication suggest the opposite. Such a contrast may be appropriately signalled in a clue:

> *Old hero's sole weakness? Yes and no (8,4)*
> *A sandwich? Hardly! (6,4)*
> *On the level? Yes and no (5)*
> *Put on view – or the opposite (8)*

BREAKING UP

Here the setter exploits the natural tendency to react to a familiar phrase as a gestalt:

> *Oscar Wilde's Miss Fairfax, for example, after school (7,5)*
> *No opera house at first in capital of state (8)*
> *Protection for head of state (6)*

Sort of china, in addition, in tea set (7)

GRAMMATICAL

An instance of a grammatical oddity is a word that has two meanings with different plurals for those meanings. This peculiarity is the basis of the clue:

You could take an iron for one of these birdies (5)

Other examples based on grammatical structure:

Had to have such a change? That's profound (7)
Turn relatively late in the day to PM, for example (10)
Easily provides an example of this (6)
Fish – importing four at the start of term (5)
Damage to part of plane it follows I have to carefully fix, for example (5,10)

RHYME AND REASON

Rhymes in an answer may provide the basis for a clue:

Traditional way to teach rhymes (5,3,4)
Accurately reproducing guy's rhymes (2-2)
Why rhymes are needed for this literary genre (3-2)
Rhyming slang for plutocrat (3,3)

LETTER-PLAY

Many words and phrases afford ways of describing them in terms of their constituent letters:

Walk in Greece – the whole length of Sparta? (4)
Like CID, but not the police, in drug investigation (5-4)
She just makes it into the first eleven (3)
Directed the leading characters, apart from the second (5)

The girl who has my letters (5)
Type either of the letters in front of you, say (4)
Add finishing touch that's sometimes seen on car (3,2,3)
Trigger-happy? Shoot two characters before I duck (4-2)
Labourer's refusal to accept work initially halved (5)

DECOYS

A classic clue I remember from long ago (but not the source) is:

A chap could attend this celebration, but never does? (4,5)

The tendency to interpret the last word as a verb (and pronounce it accordingly) rather than a noun (pronounced otherwise) makes this a really devious clue. Particularly with the intersecting letters filled in, the solution may well be found, but it would be a pity if, at this point, the solver moved on without allowing the penny to drop resoundingly. Here are some more clues in which, by one means or another, the setter lays a trap, inducing the solver to interpret a particular word in the wrong way:

Graves may be found underground here (4-6)
Feed one in residence (4)
He and I represent a couple of these (8)
As used by some poisoners? (7)
Kent gardens around centre of Sevenoaks (4)
Book supply provided in casual way (8)

and the most diabolical of the lot, in my opinion:

His, for example (9)

BACK TO FRONT

As with the last variant of anagrams discussed in Chapter 5 (see p. 73), these clues exploit a phrase that itself reads like a secondary indication for a cryptic clue. For example:

>   *Ton-up? Negative (3) [D]*

could be a clue (sound if unremarkable) for NOT. A corresponding back-to-front clue is:

>   *As fast as a motorbike, or not? (3-2) [D]*

and here are some others based on the same principle:

>   *Watch for Hun? (4-6)*
>   *Retaliation involving change of heart (3,3,3)*
>   *Vegetable – one way to make the most of pie (6)*

BEFORE YOUR VERY EYES

Edmund Akenhead, my original editor and mentor, among his many achievements, was a gifted conjuror, a lifetime member of the Magic Circle. He often compared the work of the setter with that of the illusionist: "Every cryptic crossword compiler is constantly exercising a kind of mental sleight of hand, the chief weapon in his (or her) armoury being misdirection, as it is with a conjuror". At his or her most daring, a crossword compiler waves the answer under the solver's nose:

>   *Flier last to take off or to land (7)*
>   *Imagines more than one such insect form (5)*
>   *Said whether I could provide meteorological expertise (7,3)*

I don't think one could be more blatant than:

>   *There's a girl plainly visible here (7)*

SELF-REFERENCE

Occasionally, words can be clued by reference to the crossword itself:

Network you are currently involved with (4)
Set with this, for example, to include a measure of intelligence (6)
Keen to get started on this kind of crossword (3)
What's above this in the French game? (8) [clue for 1A]
Eg two or three of what precedes or follows (6) [clue for 6D]
Disparages what this answer does (4,4) [D]

Alternatively, the reference may be to *The Times*:

Measures how long this publication is (5)
Like conformists' party line, or letters in Times? *(4)*
Paper produced from centre in Wapping – Times *(5)*
English girl absorbing Times *leader in the country (7)*

OPPORTUNISM

The setter, constantly searching for something new under the sun, is alert to fortuitous results of the juxtapositions of letters that make up our words and to other coincidences that can be exploited. The answer to the next clue could be clued in numerous ways, depending on how one decides to split it up. However, the most interesting way of treating this word, to my mind, depends on noticing that it is made up of two of the seven deadly sins, each shortened by one letter, enabling the clue:

Call to prayer curtailed sins (7)

Here is a further selection of clues that, in one way or another, exploit unusual features of words:

Blood groups, one repeated, found in tropical forest (6)
Monotonous notes about a private conversation (4-1-4)
Crew's quarters reduced by 40 per cent altogether (6)
Most parts of Fiji are scattered like this (6)
Hard-headed repetition of refusal and various points (2-8)
Warden who might have declared himself a bird-watcher (7)

OVER TO YOU

In this book, I have tried to provide you with an understanding of the rules of the game and a sound basis for playing it. As in any game, the best way to improve is by taking on strong opposition on a regular basis. Accordingly, if you want to become a competent or expert solver of *The Times* Crossword, the best way is to tackle it regularly, and, to the extent that you do not succeed in completing it, analyse the answers carefully – and if you can't work out how the answer works, try to find someone who can. To supplement this daily workout, you can read other guide-books and work on collections of crosswords from *The Times*. You will learn to take the second glance of linguistic analysis that reveals that a Labour extremist, a person with regular features, a chap who does all he can to earn a living, and a middle-aged man are a workaholic, a columnist, a swindler, and a soldier (fourth of Jacques' seven ages of man) respectively.

If you want to become a setter, I can only wish you the good luck that I had. The simple truth is that the number of people who would like to set crosswords for a daily newspaper exceeds by a large factor the number of places that exist, and, if your ambition is to join the setting team for *The Times*, you must multiply that large factor by another. My advice, based on my own experience, would be to become as familiar as possible with our style through repeated practice, starting as young as possible and persevering over many years, to study the available literature on sound cluemanship, and to try to build up a portfolio of work published in other publications. When you have done that, send examples of your work to the editor.

FINAL TEST

... in which anything goes.

ACROSS

1 How the man in the street can see what's in store for him (6-4)

6 Characters in front of queue, say, looking down on others (4)

9 As mediator, 'e is received by leader of race (10)

10 Without exception, abandoning one farm building (4)

12 Representative steps on ladder for each child (12)

15 Copy a restrictive rule, except for initial line (9)

17 Source of oil, as it happens (5)

18 Game in which county quickly succeeded (5)

19 Routine start of term – study philosopher and economist (9)

20 Pitch for performing a nocturne? (7,5)

24 Nine letters from here in return for one from abroad (4)

25 Relatively informative diagram of house (6,4)

26 Attention given to Liberal peer (4)

27 Lowest gain her doctor recorded – a stone (10)

DOWN

1 Immersing page in water produced tears (4)

2 He allowed nothing odd aboard his vessel (4)

3 Potter's work men up in a shop ordered (3-9)

4 Carefully approach second speech (5)

5 Submission to live on island in stormy ocean (9)

7 Many in parties animated with it? (4,6)

8 Long nettle leaf (4,6)

11 Top sportsman as provider of music (6,6)

13 School subject (10)

14 'e isn't involved with water! (4-6)

16 Put together a small contract, for example, with speed (9)

21 Flower-girl with hot temper (5)

22 Life? That's about right (4)

23 Construction of St Paul's 10 per cent unfinished (4)

FIRST AID SECTION

Chapter 1

Chapter 2

Chapter 3

Page 55 C _ _ _ _ _ v, S_o_n-_e_, D_a _ _ t, _l_t_e S_i _ _ _,
D_c_i _ _n_ F_l, S_ _ _ g i-_a, _ S_r_p_h _ _ _ _ _d,
_a_i_y _a_r, P_ _ _a, _ _c_o_ W_t_ _ _, J_k_ _ _,
A_i_a_ F_ _ _, U_c_e _ _ _y, B_t_, B_l_o_, _ _o_e_a_l
Page 56 T_p_ _ _ _ _y, A_ _ _a, _ _r_h, _i_q_ _ _e, R_ _ _e_t_r,
_ _ _n_w_t_ _, F_y_n_-p_ _, A_ _ _ _ _ _ d_s _ _ _k,
T_a_e_ _ _r, L_ _ _n, V_ _ _ _ _i
Page 57 D_k_ _, M_ _ _i_ge _ _ _ m_ _ _, N_ _ _t_a_c_m_ _,
_ _n_ L_s_, H_ _ _t, O_a_ _ _s, T_i_k_ _ _, L_o_ _ _e,
B_ _ _ _n _ _a P_ _ _y, L_c_ _ _w,
_e_r_e _ _e S_c_ _ _, E_ _ _x, _e_ d_e_ _, M_i_ _,
B_i_ _ _h C_l_ _ _i, N_ _ _l
Page 58 _b_d_ _ _ _, S_ _ _l_t_n, O_o_ _, N_ _s, _c_o_ _r,
C_s_ _ _d, _ _r_i_t, K_ _ _s _ _o_s, _ _ _k, O_d_ _ _s,
_ _g_t, S_ _ _n_y-e_ _ _t
Page 59 _y_h_ _ _r_s

Chapter 4

Page 64 P_ _ _a_l
Page 66 _a_h_ _ _t_n, _a_y, _ _r_s, _o_f, D_ _ _g_t, _ _c_n_,
_e_ _ _w, _ _v_s, T_ _ _h, C_ _ _ _n, _i_h, _r_p,
J_ _ _ _s_ _ _p_ _ _n, _n _ _e _ _h_r _a_d,
A_ _ _s_ t_ _ _ _a_d, _e_l-_ _ _o
Page 67 P_n_, K_ _ _, B_r_, L_ _ _n_n_, P_ _ _t_v_
Page 68 I_ _-u_e_, P_ _-h_o_e_, G_ _ _t-_r_t, R_g_ _ _y,
_o_y_h_ _ _m, _a_f, C_ _ _o_ _ _e, L_p_ _ _d,
L_ _ _s_i_e, S_ _ _ _ _q_ _, D_e_ _ _s_, _a_f-ro_ _ _,
L_ _ o_ _v_ _ _g_ _, B_ _ _-f_ _ _
Page 69 T_a_k_ _ _v_ _ _ _ _y, S_e_w_ _ _ F_ _ _s, E_o_e,
_ _ _e _f _a_, P_ _ _r _i_ _, O_ _ _r,
R_c_ _ _ _ _g_ _n_e_, M_ _ _e_ s_ _ _c, R_l_,
A_n_ _ _y, A_b_ _ _ _ _s

Chapter 5

Page 71   C_ _ _p_ _ _a
Page 72   B_ _ _u_a _ _ _a_g_e, A_f_ _ _ D_ _ _i_ _ _e,
          _ _r_n_l_i, P_o_a_o_ _ _ _, _c_ _ _l_a_t_ _,
          _e_ _e_m, R_g_ _ _t, _ _k_s_a_, S_ _ _a_a,
          I_p_e_ _ _i, W_ _ _d_ _p, N_n_e_, _p_ _ _b,
          C_ _ _ _ _h, _e_r_e B_ _ _o_
Page 73   M_l_d_ _ _, O_t_ _ _o_h, M_ _ _f_ _ _o, R_a_p_ _ _,
          D_c_ _ _l_ _, _h_a_t, O_ _ _g, _ _r_n, C_s_ _ _,
          T_ _ _l_a_, T_a_s_ _ _t, M_t_ _ _o_i, D_ _ _s_l,
          C_ _ _t_b_ _, _ m_ _ _ o_ p_ _ _a_e, A_ _ _r_a_e,
          S_ _ _h_i_s, N_ _ _f, E_ _ _m_ _ _r_ _ _i_n_

Chapter 6

Page 76   O_ _ _, S_ _ _a_ _, _ _i
Page 77   _p_ _ _a_t_, _ _ _p, U_s_ _ _t_e, V_ _ _i, _ _p_s_ _,
          _ _n_o, E_ _ _y_ _ _, A_ _ _t_t_ _, _ _c_ _, _ C_ _ _g,
          _s_ _, _ _n_m, B_ _ _ a_ _ _ e_ _ _
Page 78   _ _n_ a_d _ _ _d_e_, L_b_ _ _, _r_e, _ _e_o
Page 79   L_i, R_ _ _t, _ _c_f_ _, T_ _ _-p_ _ _, S_ _-_i, R_ _ _s,
          _e_o, O_ _ _s, _ _i_h, O_ _ _r, _i_f, O_e_ _o,
          I_ _ _r_ o_, _ _ _g_ e_r, E_ _ _l, _h_ _ _l

Chapter 7

Page 80   B_ _ _k_a_, W_ _ _s_ _ _t, _ _o_d_a_ _ _n_,
          _ _j_ _ _u_t, _i_c_v_ _ _, T_ _ _o_ _, A_ _ _f_c_ _,
          A_ _ _c_ _ _t_ _, L_ _ _n_ o_ _,
          C_ _ _ _ _f_ _r_ _ _a_k
Page 81   T_ _ _a_o_, I_a_a_e, M_ _h_ _, M_ _ _h_o_,
          M_ _ _i_ _ _t, _ _d_ _ _p_r, C_ _ _t_ _-_r_ _ _s_l,
          _ _r_t_e_ _ _n, H_ _ _t-_ _ _d_n_, _u_s_ _ d_ _ _,
          C_a_ _ _s_ _ _g_t_n, M_ _ _a_e_h, C_ _ _r_v_ _ _,
          N_ _ _p_ _

Page 82 N_t_i_s, S_ _ _a, _u_t_n, D_ _ _ _ _s, _ _i_s, A_t_,
_ _b_t, P_ _ _r_

Page 83 _ _t, _p_d_ _, S_ _ _f, D_l_ _, S_ _ _k_ _ or
R_k_ _ _s, _ _k_ _ _s, S_ _ _k_ _, T_ _ _i, E_ _ _h_n,
M_g_ _ _ _, T_ _ _n_ _a, O_ _ _r, _ _d_t

Page 84 B_ _ _, _e_f_ _ _, T_n_ _, _ _ _ _y_ _ _m

Chapter 8

Page 85 C_ _l_ _, _o_f_r, _ _ _c, _ _r_d, _e_e, F_ _ _ _h, _ _n_r,
_ _o_-h_ _

Page 86 _e_n or _a_n, _a_n, _e_n, K_ _ _ _ _a_e, _v_ _ _l_w,
P_ _ _i_ _ _n, M_s_ _ _s, _ _e_ _-r_y,
_a_ _ _p_ _o_ _

Page 87 B_ _ _n_ _r_p_ _ _ _ _, R_ _ba, _u_p, _ _a_c, C_ _ _o,
B_ _ _y_ _ _ _c, M_ _ _s, _ _o_ _t, N_ _ _e_ _a_e, _ _y_r,
_ _v_d, _o_s, R_ _ _ _d, E_e-_h_m_

Chapter 9

Page 90 E_p_ _ _b_ _, M_ _ _ _l_y, W_k_ _ _, _ _o_ _ _ _m,
M_ _ _y_ _ _, _ _a_ _ _ _t_y

Page 91 E_e_ _ _s_, _ _g_t_o_, _ _n_y, P_o_ _ _s_

Page 92 M_ _ _h_ _ _k, P_ _ _ _ _b

Page 93 B_ _ _ _ _y_, C_a_ _ _r, _ _n_y, O_r_ _, C_n_ _ _e_t,
S_e_p_ _ _, A_ _ _e_s, _ _s_ _ _s_ _ _t_r, _ _d_u_,
A_f_ _ _, C_c_ _ _ _ _, P_ _ _p_ _, N_a_ _t_i_ _,
S_ _g_ _, N_ _ _e

Page 94 C_n_ _ _t_ _, F_ _ _p_ _y, G_ _ _r_ _, H_ _ _r_ _ _o,
_u_g_ _v_ _ _, P_ _ _d, T_ _ _ _ _i, A_o_ _ _ _s,
M_n_ _ _u_ _, _ _p_d, _ _s_i, H_p_ _ _ _,
M_ _ _h_ _ _e_

Page 95 _ _o-_a, _o_h, O_o_, _ _l_r, D_ _ _, T_e_, _ _g_,
_ _n_y, _e_s, _g_ _ _a, _n_ _ _d, A_ _ _y, T_a_,
P_ _ _m_ _ _n, A_n_, _r_t, _o_s, _ _s_n, _l_e

Page 96   S_o_ _ _, E_e_, P_ _ _t_n, _ _l_y, L_ _ _t_ _ _s,
              _ _c_t_n, P_ _ _b_g_, _r_g, B_ _ _d_ M_ _ _

Page 97   M_ _ _r_ _ _y, M_ _ _f_ _ _, W_ _ _r-_ _ _o,
              B_ _ _e_m_ _ _, D_ _ _i_i_n, D_ _ _n_ _ _i_a_ c_,
              V_ _ _u_ _ _

Chapter 10

Page 99   M_ _ _a

Page 100 B_l_e_, T_ _ _y _a_e, S_p_ _ _r_, _ _g_ _ _a_e _ _b_y,
              _ _n_s, _s_ _ _e, S_ _ _p_ _ _g, M_ _ _e, _ _t_ _ _y

Page 101 _e_n, T_i_ _ _, A_ _ _ _ _y, T_ _ _c_ _ _, _ _e_t,
              R_ _ _s_g, T_ _ _a, P_ _ _-_ _o, H_ _ _h_ _ _

Page 102 P_ _-_o_, H_ _ _-_ _s_, C_ _ _-c_ _ _, F_ _ _r_p,
              R_ _ _l _ _ _y, S_ _ _s _o_ _ _g_, _ _d_m,
              P_ _ _e_ _ _b_ _ _t, _l_m_ _, M_ _ _h_ _ _a_ _ _,
              A_ _ _l_ _ _ h_ _ _, S_u_ _ _ _ _a_, L_ _ _g,
              S_ _ _e_e_, A_a_ _ _ _ _w_ _ _, H_ _ _l_ _ _,
              P_ _ _m_

Page 103 C_ _ _ _ _ _a, G_ e_ _ _, _ _t_n_ _, A_ _ _e_i_t, A_v_ _ _,
              T_ _ _a, _ _l_t _ _ _i_i_ _ _e, C_ _ _k_ _n_ t_ _ _,
              H_-_ _, S_ _-_ _ _, F_ _ _ _a_, S_o_, _ _p_ _-_a_e, _ _y,
              F_ _ _d

Page 104 _ _n_y, S_r_, C_p_ _t _ _ _ _, G_ _ _-h_, N_ _ _y,
              S_a_ _ _ _ _y, W_ _ _-c_l_ _ _, P_i_, E_e_ _ _t_,
              A_s_ _ _ _, K_e_, B_i_ _ _l, G_e_ _ _n_s

Page 105 T_ _-_p, H_ _ _-_ n_e_, _ _t _o_ t_ _, T_ _ _ _p,
              O_ _ _l_n, I_a_o, W_ _ _h_r _ _ _, T_e_ _ _a

Page 106 _r_d, C_ _ _u_, C_ _, L_ _ _o_s_, F_c_o_,
              R_ _ _ _ _w_, _ _m_ _ _, _o_d, _ _g_s, E_ _ _n_a,
              A_g_ _ _s, B_ _b_ _ _, T_ _ _-a-_ _ _e, _ _o_s_e, _o_t_d,
              _o-_o_ _ _n_e, S_ _ _n_r

SOLUTIONS AND NOTES

Chapter 1

Chum, Manor

Chapter 2

Hearsay, Syllogism, Predators, Tigress, Answer to Sphinx's riddle: man, who crawls as a baby, walks in his prime, and with a stick when old; Pavement, Herbalist, Self-Portrait, Swiss Roll, Foster-Parents, Serenader, Soft Sell, Don Juan In Hell, Tattoo, Igloo, Cars, Thunder, Atlas, Adder, Dock, Norm-Andy, Castanet, Wholesome, Hidden Poets: Gray, Moore, Byron, Pope, Dryden, Gay, Keats, Hemans; Fasten your seat belts, (Reagents, Sergeant), Estrange; Reversals: Revel, Repel, Lived, Rail, Door, Doom; Lived, Rail, Forte, Aloud, Crews

Too wise you are
Too wise you be
I see you are
Too wise for me

Abby, have you any eggs?
Yes, we have eggs.
Have you any ham?
Yes, we have ham.
Okay, I'll have ham an' eggs.

Yucca, Cabinet, Tradesmen, Narcissus, Bedsit, Curacao or Madeira, Lemon or Melon, Vandalise or Vandalize

Chapter 3

1930 Crossword: Crossword Puzzle No. 1

Across: 1 Smear 4 Penseroso 10 Mayo 11 Nomad 13 Respected 15 Sew 17 Dean 18 Diehard 21 Suspect 23 Relief 25 Soar 26 Skid 27 Tureens 30 Con 33 Immense 36 Alto 38 Umbo 39 Turtle 41 Rasping 43 Earldom 45 Tara 47 See 48 Diffident 50 Egret 51 Enid 52 Selenites 53 Total

Down: 2 Maori 3 Abashed 4 Par 5 Eyed 6 Noses 7 Evensong 8 Ostler 9 Oddity 12 Deal 14 Pause 16 Writ 18 Desk 19 Erin 20 Deuce 22 Pas 24 Front 28 Ensue 29 Ambition 31 Sled 32 Doom 33 Imp 34 Monad 35 Eras 36 Allegro 37 Brides 38 Useful 40 Tree 42 Greet 44 Opera 46 Anne 49 Tis

1940 Crossword

Across: 4 Swimsuit 9 Fashion 10 On strike 11 Crooner 12 Yourself 13 Seven 17 Tremulous 18 Abash 20 Titus 21 Desdemona 24 Susan 25 Pullmans 28 Bail out 29 Patricia 30 Astolat 31 Ringside

Down: 1 Carrier 2 Theorem 3 Poker 5 Window sash 6 Motor races 7 Unite 8 Twelfth man 13 State paper 14 Vest 15 Nursemaids 16 Golden Hind 19 Amos 22 Mullion 23 Natural 26 Luton 27 Tasso

1950 Crossword

Across: 1 Lilac 4 Chain-mail 8 Genevan 9 Nut-tree 10 Twin 11 Stamp 12 Odes 15 Steering-wheel 17 Penny-farthing 20 Elba 21 Divot 22 Door 25 Dolphin 26 Downing 27 Wednesday 28 Busts

Down: 1 Lightship 2 Lentils 3 Cave 4 Consternation 5 Nuts 6 Abridge

7 Leeks 9 Nomination day 13 Kenya 14 Swain 1 ₘₑ
Regis 18 Nibbled 19 Glories 20 Endow 23 Shoe 24 S

1965 Crossword

Across: 1 Play-pen 5 Decibel 9 Avail 10 Pompadour 11 Amelia
12 Pin-money 14 Kurds 15 Overtures 18 Tormentil 20 Ricks
22 High jump 24 Tiptop 26 Milliards 27 Usage 28 Stretch
29 Shebeen

Down: 1 Pea-jacket 2 Amateur 3 Palliasse 4 Nips 5 Demoiselle
6 Charm 7 Browner 8 Lorry 13 Route march 16 Turpitude
17 Sisyphean 19 Regular 21 Cottage 22 Hames 23 Joint
25 Asks

1980 Crossword

Across: 1 Golden Jubilee 9 Golden egg 10 Alamo 11 Loyal 12 Eton
13 Dore 15 Schisms 17 Surface 18 Filbert 20 Nest-egg
21 Eros 22 Rest 23 Athos 26 Satyr 27 Orchestra
28 The Golden Gate

Down: 1 Gaggles of geese 2 Lolly 3 Eyeglasses 4 Jeerers 5 Bugloss
6 Leaf 7 Elaborate 8 Sovereign state 14 Crustacean
16 Heliostat 19 Tremolo 20 Noticed 24 Hatta 25 Orfe

Seismic, Slipknot, Olive, Indigo, Franglais, Faute de mieux, C'est la vie,
Elevator, Aluminum (American word for it, ie, with I once extracted),
Chesterton, Chekhov, Spoon-fed, Diarist (references to *Diary of a
Nobody*, and John Evelyn), *Blithe Spirit* (comedy Noel Coward
quoting "Hail to thee, blithe spirit from Shelley's *Ode to a Skylark*),
Decline and Fall, Shangri-la (hidden Buddhist lama paradise in James
Hilton's *Lost Horizon*, Hilton = Milton with initial change), *A
Shropshire Lad*, *Vanity Fair*, Petra (reference to "A rose-red city half as
old as time" in Dean Burgon's *Petra*), Doctor Watson, Jekyll, *Animal
Farm*, Unclearly (reference to Edward Lear's poem *Incidents in the life*

of Uncle Arly), Beth (second letter in Hebrew and Phoenician alphabets; Meg, Jo, Beth and Amy were the children in the March family in *Little Women* by Louisa M. Alcott), Belloc (reference to "The chief defect of Henry King/Was chewing little bits of string" from *Cautionary Tales*), Stonewall ("Stone walls do not a prison make" in Richard Lovelace's *To Althea, from prison*), Tipperary, At sea, North, Misquote (the correct quotations are "Lay on, Macduff" in *Macbeth* and "fresh woods, and pastures new" in Milton's *Lycidas*), Red setter, Drinkwater, Frying-pan, All in a day's work, Traveller, Latin (sex = 6), Vivaldi, Dukas (wrote *The Sorcerer's Apprentice*), *Marriage à la mode* (sequence of pictures by Hogarth; reference to "Daisy, Daisy, give me your answer do ... It won't be a stylish marriage"), Nightwatchmen, *Mona Lisa*, Holst, Oranges, Thinking (kings known as Charles the Fat and Louis the Fat, respectively), Leonine, Boston Tea Party, Lucknow, George the Second (last English monarch to lead troops in battle), Essex, Dead Sea (lowest place on Earth's surface, about 1300 ft below sea level), Maine, British Columbia (capital of which is Victoria), Nepal, Obedient, Singleton, Ovoid (Fabergé famous for jewellery in form of eggs), News, Scholar (so-called scholar's mate in chess, on white's fourth move), Castled, Geraint, King's Cross (the cross on the king in a chess set is the highest part of any piece), Rook, Oddness, Eight, Seventy-eight (sum of the numbers from 1 to 12), Pythagoras

Chapter 4

Portable, Washington, Gamy, Lords, Loaf, Draught, Second, Yellow, Dives, Teeth, Cut in, High, Trap, Job description, On the other hand, Across the board, Well-to-do, Pink, Kilt, Bore, Learning, Positive, Ice-cube, Pea-shooter, Ghost-write, Regency, Polytheism, Calf, Chocolate, Lipread, Landslide, Soliloquy, Duellist, Half-crowns (D-Day not June 6, 1944 but February 15, 1971 when decimal coinage was introduced), Law of averages, Baby-face, Thanksgiving Day, Sherwood Forest, Elope, Isle of Man, Power line, Oscar, Recording angel, Maiden speech, Rill, Amnesty, Albatross (score of three under par in golf; reference to Coleridge's *The Rime of the Ancient Mariner*)

Chapter 5

Dante Gabriel Rossetti, Grover Cleveland, Madam Curie, Ralph Waldo Emerson, Roald Amundsen, Misfortune, Committees, Conversation, Decimal point, Endearment, Cleopatra, Bermuda Triangle, Alfred Doolittle, Cor anglais, Protagonist, Schoolmaster, Te Deum, Regulate, Pakistan, Sultana, Impresario, World Cup, Nansen, Aplomb, Cheetah, George Borrow (anagram of WB, eg, eg, or, or, or), Melodist, Ostrogoths, Manifesto, Reappear, Decathlon, Wheat, Oflag, Turin, Casino, Tirolean, Transient, Metropolis, Damosel, Constable, A mess of pottage, Alternate, Smash hits, Nod off, *Enigma Variations*

First Test

Across: 1 Roast (triple definition; pan = criticise severely = roast) 4 Analgesia (anagram) 9 Lullabies (cryptic definition) 10 Angle (double definition) 11 Starting price (anagram) 14 Oust (anagram) 15 Striptease (anagram) 18 Cartridges (anagram) 19 Dido (double definition) 21 Channel Tunnel (cryptic definition) 24 Alibi (anagram) 25 Desert pea (anagram) 27 Right-hand (double definition) 28 Needs (cryptic definition)

Down: 1 Rolls Royce (anagram) 2 Awl (anagram; last = cobbler's tool) 3 Tracts (double definition) 4 Alienated (anagram) 5 Aesop (cryptic definition) 6 Gladiate (cryptic definition; second half of a crossword = sword) 7 Segregation (anagram) 8 Axes (double definition) 12 Abstracting (double definition) 13 New Orleans (inverse anagram; Salerno = new (ie, anagram of) Orleans) 16 Idealised (anagram; with Ed. tacked on to the end) 17 Organist (double anagram; "As to *Air on G string*" contains the letters of the answer twice) 20 Outrun (cryptic definition) 22 Nadia (anagram; better answer than Aidan) 23 Fair (triple definition) 26 Pie (double definition; reference to "Four and twenty blackbirds baked in a pie")

Chapter 6

Oslo, Smetana, Eli, Ipso facto, Ship, Unsheathe, Verdi, Riposte, Rondo, Essayist, Annotator, Nacho, I Ching, Esau, Venom, Bath and Wells, Pins and needles, Libyan, Erne, Credo, Laic, Relit, Pacific, Tone-poem, Sci-fi, Roots, Leno, Omens, Edith, Order, Tiff, Overdo (hidden in Dover Dover), Intercom, *King Lear*, Ethel, Chisel

Chapter 7

Blackcap, Windswept, Broadcasting, Major suit, Discovery, Tedious, Artifacts, Anarchistic, Laying out, Cardiff Arms Park, Testator, Imamate (Fletcher Christian, mate on *Bounty*), Mayhem, Matchbox, Mendicant, Kidnapper, Counter-proposal, First reading, Heart-rending, Cuts a dash, Charles Laughton, Marrakech, Contravene, Notepad, Nitwits, Siena, Euston, Delibes, Aries, Alto, Sabot, Pierre, But, Spider, Serif, Delos, Stinker or Reknits, Reknits, Stinker, Tennis, Erewhon, Megaton, Tenon saw, Odder, Godot, Boob, Deified, Tenet, Malayalam

Chapter 8

Choler, Coffer, Bloc, World, Fete, Finish, Tenor, Know-how, Rein or Rain, Rain, Rein, Kittiwake, Overflow, Philistine, Mistrust, Steel-Grey, Gallup Poll, Banana republic, Rumba, Rump, Isaac, Curio, Belly dance, Moses, Frost, Notre Dame, Buyer, David, Does, Rowed, Eye-rhyme

Second Test

Across: 1 For example (addition and insertion; X in fore + ample) 7 Onus (hidden) 9 Sequence (homophone; sounds like seek whence) 10 Really (addition; re + ally) 11 Callas (homophone; sounds like callous) 12 Insights (homophone; sounds like incites) 13 View (hidden) 15 Legitimate (addition; leg it + I + mate) 18 Antonymous (insertion; t in anonymous) 20 Neon (hidden) 21 Stressed (reversal) 24 Invent (addition; in + vent) 26 Strait (homophone; sounds like straight) 27 Acid rain (addition; ac + I + drain) 28 Once (hidden) 29 Discretely (homophone; sounds like discreetly)

Down: 2 Operation (insertion; era in option) 3 Equal (hidden) 4 Aunt Sally (hidden) 5 Peeking (homophone; sounds like peaking) 6 Earns (homophone; sounds like urns) 7 Orangeman (addition and reversal; orang + name reversed) 8 Unlit (addition; un + lit (French)) 14 Wholesale (homophone; sounds like hole sail) 16 Testifier (hidden) 17 Thornbill (addition; t + hornbill) 19 Ordeals (addition; or + deals) 22 Titan (homophone; sounds like tighten) 23 Sited (homophone; sounds like sighted and cited) 25 Verst (hidden)

Chapter 9

Euphorbia, Misplay, Woking, Egotism, Moneyed, Peasantry, Exercise, Negation, Honey, Progress, Matchlock, Proverb, Beta rays, Chatter, Wendy (Wendy Darling, in *Peter Pan*), Oared, Continent, Sweeping, Artless, Unsatisfactory, Ardour, Alfred, Cockney, Prosper, Near thing, Shogun, Noble, Contented, Frippery, Generic, Hey presto, Hung over, Plead, Trotski, Amorous, Mannequin, Sapid, Sushi, Hapless, Manchester, Hoo-ha, Cosh, Oboe, Idler, Demo, Trek, Edgy, Dandy, Tees, Uganda, Ennead, Apery, Thai, Ptarmigan, Arne, Brat, Togs, Rosin, Clue, Scorch, Ewer (remove th and at from the water), Phaeton, Relay, Locations, Nicotine, Plumbago, Drug, Bloody Mary, Man Friday, Manifest, Water-polo, Bridesmaid, Dietician, Disinheritance, Virtuosi

Chapter 10

Mocha, Billet, Tipsy cake, Sapphire, Nightmare Abbey, Kings, Estate, Stripling, Maybe, Utterly, Hewn, Thirst, Allergy, Tramcar, Cheat, Redesign, Tartar, Pooh-pooh, Hot shots, Pom-pom, Hush-hush, Cock-crow, Flytrap, Royal Navy, Swiss Cottage, Madam, Presentability,

Blimey, Merchantable, Achilles heel, Square meal, Lying, Screened, Academy Award (Gwendolen Fairfax in *The Importance of Being Earnest* is a ward), Honolulu, Panama, Chelsea, Geese, Intense, Abbreviate, Adverb, Tetra, Split infinitive, Chalk and talk, Hi-fi, Sci-fi, Fat cat, Stoa, Upper-case, Kay, Faced, Mandy, Sort, Cap it all, Gung-ho, Navvy, Stag party, Wine-cellar, Paid, Elements (He = Helium, I = Iodine), Arsenic (As = Arsenic), Knew, Blithely, Greetings, Ton-up, Half-hunter, Tit for tat, Turnip, Ortolan, Imago, Weather eye, Theresa, Grid, Clique, Cry, Lacrosse, Factor, Runs down, Times, Toed, Pages, Estonia, Angelus, Baobab, Tete-a-tete, Fo'c's'le, Dotted, No-nonsense, Spooner (Warden of New College, Oxford, famous word-botcher)

Final Test

Across: 1 Window-shop (cryptic definition) 6 Atop (letter-play and inverse homophone; a to p, letters before q, which sounds like queue) 9 Peacemaker (insertion; e in pacemaker) 10 Barn (subtraction; bar none – one) 12 Spokesperson (addition; spokes + per + son) 15 Imitation (subtraction; limitation – 1) 17 Olive (first letter and addition; o + live) 18 Chess (addition; Ches + s) 19 Treadmill (addition; t + read + Mill) 20 Playing field (double definition; John Field (1782–1837) was an Irish pianist and composer best known for his nocturnes, a form that he invented) 24 Iota (letter-play and reversal; a to i, reversed) 25 Family tree (cryptic definition) 26 Earl (addition; ear + 1) 27 Nethermost (addition; net + her + MO + st)

Down: 1 Wept (insertion; p in wet (= water, as verb)) 2 Noah (cryptic definition; Genesis 7:9 "There went in two and two unto Noah into the Ark, the male and the female") 3 One-upmanship (anagram; Stephen Potter (1900–69), author of *One-upmanship*) 4 Stalk (addition; s + talk) 5 Obeisance (hybrid of addition, insertion, anagram; (be + Is) in anagram of ocean) 7 Team spirit (hybrid of insertion, anagram, addition, & lit.; M in anagram of parties + it, & lit.) 8 Pine needle (addition; pine + needle) 11 Record player (double definition) 13 Discipline (double definition) 14 Wine-taster (anagram & lit.) 16 Integrate (addition; I NT + eg + rate) 21 Irish (addition; Iris + h) 22 Brio (insertion & lit.; r in bio) 23 Tent (subtraction; tenth − h, St Paul was a tent-maker)

REFERENCES

Arnot, M. (1982). *A history of the crossword puzzle*. London: Macmillan.

Augarde, T. (1986). *The Oxford guide to word games*. Oxford: Oxford University Press.

Barnard, D. St.P. (1963). *Anatomy of the crossword*. London: Camelot Press.

Bergerson, H. W. (1973). *Palindromes and anagrams*. New York: Dover.

Bierce, A. (1993). *The devil's dictionary*. New York: Dover [originally published in 1911].

Buranelli, P., Hartswick, F. G. & Petherbridge, M. (1924). *The cross word puzzle book*. New York: Plaza Publishing Company. [Reissued in 1974 by Arno Press, New York]

Cash, A. (Ed.). (1980). *The Penguin book of The Times 50th anniversary crosswords*. London: Penguin.

Dudeney, H. E. (1968). *300 best word puzzles*. New York: Charles Scribner's Sons.

Macnutt, D. S. (1966). *Ximenes on the art of the crossword*. London: Methuen.

Manley, D. (1986). *Chambers crossword manual*. Edinburgh: Chambers.

Mathers, E. P. (1934). *The Torquemada puzzle book*. London: Gollancz.

Millington, R. (1974). *The strange world of the crossword*. Walton-on-Thames: M. & J. Hobbs.

Polya, G. (1945). *How to solve it*. Princeton: Princeton University Press.

Ritchie, A. F. (1949). *Armchair crosswords*. London: Warne.

Robins, A. (1975). *Teach yourself crosswords*. London: Hodder & Stoughton. [Reissued in 1981 as *The ABC of crosswords* by Corgi Books, London]

Stoppard, T. (1978). *Every good boy deserves favour* and *Professional foul*. London: Faber & Faber.

Other *Times* and *Sunday Times* crossword publications

The Times Crossword Book 1
ISBN 0-00-710833-8 £5.99

The Times Crossword Book 2
ISBN 0-00-711581-4 £5.99

The Times Crossword Masterclass
ISBN 0-7230-1059-5 £6.99

The Times 2 Crossword Book 1
ISBN 0-00-711078-2 £3.99

The Sunday Times Concise Crossword Book 1
ISBN 0-00-711153-3 £3.99

The Sunday Times Cryptic Crossword Book 1
ISBN 0-00-711075-8 £5.99